Developing a
Residency Program

PRACTICAL GUIDES FOR LIBRARIANS

⊚ About the Series

This innovative series written and edited for librarians by librarians provides authoritative, practical information and guidance on a wide spectrum of library processes and operations.

Books in the series are focused, describing practical and innovative solutions to a problem facing today's librarian and delivering step-by-step guidance for planning, creating, implementing, managing, and evaluating a wide range of services and programs.

The books are aimed at beginning and intermediate librarians needing basic instruction/ guidance in a specific subject and at experienced librarians who need to gain knowledge in a new area or guidance in implementing a new program/service.

⊚ About the Series Editors

The **Practical Guides for Librarians** series was conceived and edited by M. Sandra Wood, MLS, MBA, AHIP, FMLA, Librarian Emerita, Penn State University Libraries from 2014-2017.

M. Sandra Wood was a librarian at the George T. Harrell Library, the Milton S. Hershey Medical Center, College of Medicine, Pennsylvania State University, Hershey, PA, for over thirty-five years, specializing in reference, educational, and database services. Ms. Wood received an MLS from Indiana University and an MBA from the University of Maryland. She is a fellow of the Medical Library Association and served as a member of MLA's Board of Directors from 1991 to 1995.

Ellyssa Kroski assumed editorial responsibilities for the series beginning in 2017. She is the director of Information Technology at the New York Law Institute as well as an award-winning editor and author of 36 books including *Law Librarianship in the Digital Age* for which she won the AALL's 2014 Joseph L. Andrews Legal Literature Award. Her ten-book technology series, *The Tech Set* won the ALA's Best Book in Library Literature Award in 2011. Ms. Kroski is a librarian, an adjunct faculty member at Drexel and San Jose State University, and an international conference speaker. She has just been named the winner of the 2017 Library Hi Tech Award from the ALA/LITA for her long-term contributions in the area of Library and Information Science technology and its application.

1. *How to Teach: A Practical Guide for Librarians* by Beverley E. Crane
2. *Implementing an Inclusive Staffing Model for Today's Reference Services* by Julia K. Nims, Paula Storm, and Robert Stevens
3. *Managing Digital Audiovisual Resources: A Practical Guide for Librarians* by Matthew C. Mariner
4. *Outsourcing Technology: A Practical Guide for Librarians* by Robin Hastings
5. *Making the Library Accessible for All: A Practical Guide for Librarians* by Jane Vincent
6. *Discovering and Using Historical Geographic Resources on the Web: A Practical Guide for Librarians* by Eva H. Dodsworth and L. W. Laliberté

Developing a Residency Program
A Practical Guide for Librarians

Lorelei Rutledge
Jay L. Colbert
Anastasia Chiu
Jason Alston

PRACTICAL GUIDES FOR LIBRARIANS, NO. 63

ROWMAN & LITTLEFIELD
Lanham • Boulder • New York • London

Published by Rowman & Littlefield
An imprint of The Rowman & Littlefield Publishing Group, Inc.
4501 Forbes Boulevard, Suite 200, Lanham, Maryland 20706
www.rowman.com

6 Tinworth Street, London, SE11 5AL, United Kingdom

British Library Cataloguing in Publication Information Available

Library of Congress Cataloging-in-Publication Data

Names: Rutledge, Lorelei, 1985– author. | Colbert, Jay, 1993– author. | Chiu, Anastasia, 1987– author. | Alston, Jason Kelly, author.
Title: Developing a residency program : a practical guide for librarians / Lorelei Rutledge, Jay Colbert, Anastasia Chiu, Jason Alston.
Description: Lanham : Rowman & Littlefield, [2019] | Series: Practical guides for librarians ; 63 | Includes bibliographical references and index.
Identifiers: LCCN 2018056385 (print) | LCCN 2019001610 (ebook) | ISBN 9781538116968 (Electronic) | ISBN 9781538116951 (pbk. : alk. paper)
Subjects: LCSH: Interns (Library science)—United States. | Academic librarians—In-service training—United States. | Minority librarians—Recruiting—United States.
Classification: LCC Z682.4.I58 (ebook) | LCC Z682.4.I58 .R88 2019 (print) | DDC 023—dc23
LC record available at https://lccn.loc.gov/2018056385

Contents

Figures and Tables

⑨ Figures

⑨ Tables

Preface

Although library residency programs have been around for a while, few resources are available that offer practical tips and concrete suggestions for developing and running a residency program. As current and past residents and coordinators, we wanted to create such a resource for other institutions considering developing such a program. The information in this book draws largely from our own experiences and also includes scholarly literature when appropriate. During the composition of the book, we also conducted an Institutional Review Board–approved study asking former and current residents and coordinators to complete a survey about their experiences. We also asked study participants to send us residency documentation, however they defined it, and invited them to contribute short autoethnographic essays about their experiences as residents or coordinators. The results of this study are included throughout this book. The autoethnographies we received are included through the chapters.

Organization

Chapter 1 describes the development of residency programs in librarianship, focusing on the different types of residencies available. The chapter also explores the goals of library residencies and how they differ from internships. This chapter, although not comprehensive, is useful for gaining background knowledge about library residency programs. Chapter 2 focuses on the benefits of hosting a residency for the profession, the institution, and the resident, providing concrete feedback about potential hurdles to developing such a program and how to address them. Chapter 3 focuses on building support for a residency program, helping readers identify key stakeholders whose support they need to develop the program, write a proposal for a program that describes in detail how such a program will benefit the stakeholders, and develop a plan to share the proposal and communicate with stakeholders throughout program development.

The next section focuses on the key processes of preparing to host a resident. Chapter 4 describes how to use backward design principles to develop clear and useful professional development opportunities, as well as how to develop a project structure for the resident. Chapter 5 describes how to build an administrative structure for the program that supports the resident and clarifies his or her role in the organization. Chapter 6 is about developing an appropriate and timely hiring process that avoids bias. Chapter 7 offers best practices for familiarizing staff with the purpose and goals of the residency before the resident comes, sharing information with the resident about their first projects and the benefits available to them, and completing logistical and operational tasks. Chapter 8 describes how to create an appropriate onboarding process for the resident. Chapter 9 focuses on how to develop assessments for various aspects of the residency, while chapter 10 makes suggestions about how to support the resident during the final stages of the residency and after the residency is complete. Although the book is organized sequentially, each chapter is self-contained and stands on its own.

We hope that this book will help our readers and their institutions consider starting a residency program or revitalizing a current or lapsed program. Such programs, as this book will describe, have potential to offer numerous benefits to the library profession, hosting institutions and stakeholders, and the residents. We also hope that our experiences, as well as the experiences of our contributors and those in the literature we cite, will help you as you develop an amazing residency program.

Acknowledgments

We would like to thank all of our colleagues who generously contributed their time and expertise to this book. In particular, we thank all of those who participated in our research by answering our survey questionnaire, contributed documents or autoethnographies for this work, or provided other support, including Mary Abler, Andrea Anesi, Annie Bélanger, Ken Brecher, Tallie Casucci, Joanna Chen Cham, Erika Church, Madison Donnelly, Gerald Holmes, Sarah LeMire, John Loughton, Thura Mack, Cynthia Mediavilla, Alfred Mowdood, Allyson Mower, Evangela Q. Oates, Hannah Lee Park, Alexandra Provo, Marje K. Schuetze-Coburn, Catherine Soehner, and those who have chosen to remain anonymous.

What Is a Library Residency Program?

IF YOU FOLLOW ANY library-related listservs, you may have noticed the increasing number of job postings recruiting for residency programs. More and more, academic libraries in particular are creating positions for new graduates of library schools, particularly those from diverse backgrounds. Many of these positions center around student engagement or are even project based. If you are considering creating a residency program at your library, however, it will be helpful to know more specifics about what options you have and what other institutions host these programs. This chapter serves as an introduction to library residency programs and their history.

What Is a Library Residency Program?

But what is a library residency program, and how does it differ from graduate internships and fellowships? This seems to be a common point of confusion among librarians; a frequently asked question of the Association of College and Research Libraries' (ACRL) Residency Interest Group (RIG) FAQ page is "A residency program . . . you mean like an internship?"[1]

In order to help bring clarity to this difference, RIG has compiled three definitions to differentiate residencies from internships and fellowships. These definitions, summarized from an ARL Spec Kit,[2] are:

- Internship: Preprofessional (Pre-MLS) work experience that takes place during graduate work but preceding the terminal degree.
- Residency: Postdegree work experience designed as an entry-level program for recent graduates of an MLS program.
- Fellowship: An experience designed to assist librarians who already have some professional experience in developing an area of expertise or managerial skills.

The key difference between these three types of work experience programs is when they take place in a librarian's career. Library residency programs, as stated above, are designed as *postdegree experiences, normally within the first few years after the master's degree has been earned.*[3]

Types of Library Residency Programs

Although the most common type of library residency program is for those interested in academic librarianship (particularly reference and/or instruction), library residency programs can happen in any type of library; indeed, even academic library residency programs show great variety. In order to build a list of the types and elements of existing library residency programs, we analyzed years of job ads posted on the RIG website. Based on these job ads and the ACRL Diversity Alliance[4] website, there are approximately sixty active library residency programs in the United States and Canada. The categories of library residency programs, found in appendix A, categorizes known existing programs in the following types. Note that a single program can and probably will fit into more than one category, as the categories may overlap.

- Cohort residents,
- Diversity residency and whether or not that program is part of the ACRL Diversity Alliance,
- Rotation/holistic projects and placements,
- Single residents,
- Subject-specific projects and placements, and
- Type of library, academic or otherwise.

Cohort Residency Programs

A cohort residency program, like the North Carolina State University Libraries Fellows program, is one where multiple residents are hired at one time, forming a cohort; rarely, a single resident will be hired each year, causing a cohort overlap. Based on the job postings and residency map on the ACRL RIG page, there are approximately twenty known residency programs that hire residents in a cohort group. A possible benefit to cohort groups is shared experience and sense of community, where residents learn, work, and grow professionally together. In one study, former diversity residents state, "Serving in a cohort was beneficial because the members of the cohort were able to provide each other with emotional support and bounce ideas off of one another."[5] Cohorts can also provide a supportive environment for cross-training and mutual learning[6] as well as support and community for diversity residents of color.[7] Alston stresses that although there is evidence of the positive outcomes of residency cohorts, there is not enough data to suggest that single residents lose out significantly; indeed, his research participants who were single residents often had similar experiences to those in cohorts. The known benefits of cohorts in residencies rely on the residents choosing to support each other in the residency experience; it should not be assumed that this will always be the case. The budget needed to hire that many people at a time could cause a lower salary or position status, as well as a sustainability issue.

Diversity Residency Programs

The problematic lack of diversity, racial, ethnic, and otherwise, in librarianship is well-documented in the scholarly literature.[8] For example, according to the Association of Research Libraries (ARL) 2014–2015 Annual Salary Survey, only "14.8% of the professional staff in US ARL university libraries (including law and medical libraries) belong to one of the four non-Caucasian categories for which ARL keeps records."[9] Although there are various statistics for the number of librarians with minoritized backgrounds, primarily racial and ethnic minority librarians, retention rate statistics are few and far between. However, much anecdotal evidence and emerging scholarship shows that many librarians of color end up leaving the field due to various explicit and implicit barriers, such as hostile environments.[10] According to Trevar Riley-Reid, these barriers for academic librarians can include pressures, obstacles, and biases in the tenure process, a problem that is also well-documented by Damasco and Hodges,[11] as well as the fact that faculty of color are often few and far between in an organization, which causes them to be treated as "other" and engenders feelings of isolation.[12]

Residency programs can be one way to recruit and retain librarians from marginalized groups. Diversity residency programs are designed to help new-career librarians get started in academic librarianship when they might otherwise have trouble getting an academic job. Some programs specifically focus on race or ethnicity, and others use multiple axes of diversity, including gender, sexual orientation, or ability, among others. Though multiple studies have shown that white women make up the majority of librarians, that majority is not as pronounced in academic librarianship:

> Men are still more likely to hold higher administrative positions, have more power and job security, and experience less stress and discrimination in the workplace than women. According to the American Library Association's "Diversity Counts," 83 percent of all "credentialed librarians" are women. The most recent Association of Research Libraries (ARL) Salary Survey reveals that 58 percent of leaders of ARL libraries are women. While this number represents a majority of leaders, it is barely a majority and not proportional to the percentage of women in the profession as a whole.[13]

Based on the RIG job ads, there are approximately forty diversity residencies, thirty-eight of which were at ACRL Diversity Alliance libraries during 2017–2018.

Rotation Residency Programs

As the name suggests, in programs of this type, the resident or residents "rotate" around the departments of the library or around different subject specialties. The purpose of these programs is not only to give a holistic view of academic librarianship to the residents but also to help them find an area they are interested in, if they do not already have a career interest planned. A trend in these programs is to rotate only the first year, while the second year or possibly third year is dedicated to one area or even a capstone project. Based on the RIG job ads, approximately twenty library residency programs follow this model.

Single Resident Programs

Instead of hiring multiple residents at once, such as in the cohort type, these programs hire one librarian at a time. Depending on the program, this single resident may or may not be given faculty status, and the position might be embedded in a department. Based on the RIG job ads, approximately thirty library residency programs are known to hire only a single resident at a time.

Subject-Specific Residency Programs

On the opposite axis of the rotation residency is the subject residency. These programs hire residents to fill a specific staffing need within the library. For instance, many residency job postings from the past few years are for instruction, digital humanities, or student engagement. These residencies can be helpful as far as consistency and sustainability of work in these areas is concerned: as long as the program exists, you know there will be a resident librarian working in that subject. Out of the known residency programs, approximately thirty hire a resident to only work in one department or have one focus.

Type of Library

The trend, it seems, is for residency programs to operate in academic libraries for recent graduates interested in pursuing a career in academic librarianship. However, this is certainly not the case always. After academic libraries, the next most popular library type that hosts residencies is government libraries, such as the National Library of Medicine, and following that are archives, independent research libraries, or otherwise special libraries. As of 2018, we found no public libraries offering residencies.

History of Library Residency Programs

For more than fifty years, libraries have been hosting postgraduates of library science programs in order to introduce new librarians to the field. In fact, the oldest residency program is still in operation. In 1957, the National Library of Medicine created an internship program, which changed into the Associate Fellowship Program in 1966. As well as getting excellent job experience as a health sciences librarian, the participating fellows also follow a "curriculum" composed of self-directed study, research, or evaluation project experiences. Although the program is only one year long, and that year contains the curriculum, there is an optional second year where the fellow gets a field placement. According to the U.S. National Library of Medicine website, more than two hundred librarians have participated in this program.[14]

Although the National Library of Medicine's official fellowship program began in 1966, the idea of a post-master's training program has existed in professional discourse since 1919, with the Williamson Report. This report, completed in 1923 by Dr. Charles Williamson by request of the Carnegie Corporation of New York, examined the state of library training programs. According to this report, most programs prior to 1923 were one-year courses that contained some field experience. Based on these findings, the report recommended that a "second year of advanced study in a specialized field" be added to complement the first year of experience.[15] Williamson cited medical internships as the inspiration for this addition, an inspiration that still affects our programs today. This report further inspired the American Library Association's Board of Education for Librarianship to study library internships, leading Francis St. John to recommend various committees and policies to implement functional library training programs.

After the Williamson Report, the literature about post-master's residency programs vanishes—although the programs continued to be developed, including the NLM Fellowship and the Library of Congress (LC) intern program—until this 1980 article, which detailed the early stages of "intern" programs at academic libraries, which today we would classify as residency programs. It was not until the late 1980s and early 1990s that library residency programs were used to increase the number of minority professionals in academic research libraries.[16] This issue is further discussed in *Diversity in Libraries: Academic Residency Programs*,[17] which shares the experiences of both residency administrators and residents. The directory of programs in this work lists thirty-four active programs, seventeen of which are minority focused; of these programs, the majority were started between 1995 and 2000.

Current Programs

The popularity and sustainability of residency programs have always been in flux. Although the very first program is still active, many libraries have started residencies only to stop them, and some even start them again. Currently, out of the almost eighty known programs, approximately sixty are currently active. Due to the fact that established residency programs may cease and then come back in different forms, it is difficult to get an accurate timeline of the development of residency programs, except for the ACRL Diversity Alliance mentioned below. Of all the current residencies, diversity residencies are by far the most popular and indeed the most written about, and most of those diversity residencies are members of the ACRL Diversity Alliance. You can find a complete list of active residencies at the time of this publication in appendix A.

The ACRL Diversity Alliance

On October 11, 2016, the executive director of ACRL announced the launch of the ACRL Diversity Alliance, a program which began with an initiative from founding members American University, the University of Iowa, Virginia Tech, and West Virginia

University. The four founding members announced their first residents in the summer and fall of 2015. During the 2016 ALA Annual Conference, the ACRL board of directors approved the program. The purpose of this program is to "unite academic libraries who share a commitment to increase the hiring pipeline of qualified, talented individuals from underrepresented racial and ethnic groups." In order to become a member of the Alliance, academic libraries must create one or more residency positions and be committed to increasing representation of minority and minoritized groups in librarianship. "Diversity is a core organizational value in ACRL's Plan for Excellence," said ACRL president Irene M. H. Herold of the University of Hawai'i at Mānoa. "This initiative aligns with the new goal area of New Roles and Changing Landscapes and the goal area of Value of Academic Libraries objective to support libraries in advancing issues of equity, access, diversity, and inclusion. With the launch of the ACRL Diversity Alliance, we put further work into action to advance our goals."[18]

In 2017, thirty-six academic libraries in the United States and Canada were members of the Diversity Alliance. That number has so far decreased in 2018 to thirty-four. Of those thirty-six members in 2017, eleven dropped in 2018 with nine new programs joining. Indeed, the majority of currently active residencies (thirty-six out of sixty) are currently or have been members of the ACRL Diversity Alliance, with only three more institutions having diversity residencies independent of the program.

As this chapter illustrates, librarianship has a long history of using residencies to promote the growth and development of the profession. There are numerous types of residencies that function for different purposes. In the following chapters, we will describe best practices for implementing a residency program at your own institution.

AN URBAN PUBLIC LIBRARY RESIDENCY PROGRAM
by Mary Abler

The first time I walked into Los Angeles Public Library's (LAPL) Central Library in downtown Los Angeles, I was struck by the solemnity of the older building. Though there is a modern portion that was added to the back of the building when it was renovated in 1993, the classic architecture of the front entrance and the quiet, cool corridor that opened up into the lobby connecting to other corridors felt like hallowed ground. The libraries I had come to know myself were modern or quaint, not stately and grand like this one. I was immediately taken in and couldn't believe that I was about to interview for a job that felt perfect, as an Innovation Leadership Resident in the first public library residency program in the country.

I had just graduated from library school, having spent the previous four years as a part-time student while working at Friends of the San Francisco Public Library as a community organizer and fund raiser. I was eager to get started applying my passion for urban libraries, and the opportunity to work in one of the largest urban libraries in the country in this unique role was almost more than I could hope for. But the interview went well, and a month later I had moved to Los Angeles and started my job.

The Innovation Leadership Program (ILP) was the perfect introduction to urban public library work. Most entry-level jobs are just that—an entry job into the profession, where you perform one role until you transfer or promote. But urban librarianship is such an incredibly diverse profession; large libraries have hundreds of employees, scores of branches, and numerous departments and serve the entirety of the population. The ILP allowed me, within the course of two years, to observe and engage with the myriad communities that LAPL serves, while also exploring the behind-the-scenes work that keeps the library running. I was also able to take my passion of library outreach to diverse communities and delve more deeply into it than I ever would have been able to in a typical entry-level position. In addition, due to the unique nature of the role, I was granted a level of access and support that allowed me to connect with administration and to travel to visit other innovative library systems across the country. The ILP cemented my passion for urban libraries and gave me a broad skill set that has accelerated my career.

Though the ILP was discontinued after my residency, I know that it had a lasting impact on LAPL. During the program, our cohort traveled to several innovative library systems throughout the country to observe and to bring ideas back to our community. Some of these visits and ideas led to the Innovation Conversation Series, where we invited leaders in the field to LAPL for a staff training experience. This series continued for several years, bringing outside-the-box thinking to all staff, not just those that were involved in the program.

The second year of our residency was spent creating a project to benefit the library, and I chose to explore nontraditional outreach through a project called the Unexpected Library Project. For a year, I led a group of staff to do outreach throughout the city in unexpected locations like bars, a train station, and public gatherings. But unlike most outreach, rather than standing behind a table, we used wi-fi hotspots and tablets to be mobile and engaging. We were able to sign folks up on the spot for library cards and demonstrate the use of our eMedia resources. Much of this work continues to this day with bilingual outreach librarians in each region and through the outreach work of my mentor in the Central Library. And I have a project in my professional portfolio that indicates a mastery of a skill set and a level of expertise well beyond most librarians with as many years of post-MLIS employment.

Participating in the ILP was all about making connections: with other libraries, with the community, and with leaders in our field. These connections were the most valuable part of my residency experience and have helped me immensely in my career. When I was unable to be hired by LAPL immediately after my residency due to the fact that the civil service register was not open yet, I was able to use my connections to find a contract position with a library cooperative. Also, because I had made connections in the librarians' union at LAPL, I was invited to attend an interview practice session that helped me prepare for all future interviews.

I believe that being an Innovation Leadership Resident has made me a stronger and more skilled library professional. I understand the inner workings of a large public library in a way that I never would have in such a short amount of time, and I have developed project management, leadership, and change management skills that have set me apart from other candidates. Most importantly, I am a more passionate advocate for the value of urban public libraries and the services that we provide to our communities.

⑥ Key Points

- Library residency programs are an opportunity for early-career credentialed librarians to learn on-the-job skills, not just graduate internships under a different name.
- These programs are designed to give new-career librarians the skills they need to succeed in their chosen field of librarianship while under supervision and mentorship.
- Library residency programs can fall into several different categories based on structure, purpose, and other factors.
- The majority of library residency programs are diversity residencies, with the majority of those claiming membership in the ACRL Diversity Alliance.

⑥ Notes

1. Association of College & Research Libraries Residency Interest Group, "FAQ—Residency Interest Group," *Residency Interest Group: An Interest Group of the Association of College & Research Libraries*, 2018, acrl.ala.org/residency/faq-2/.

2. Julie Brewer, ed., *Internship, Residency, and Fellowship Programs in ARL Libraries* (Washington, D.C.: Association of Research Libraries, Office of Management Services, 1992).

3. However, at least three residencies are given the label of fellowship. There seems to be some overlap in how these labels are applied, and for our purposes, we have included fellowships that fit the definition of residencies.

4. American Library Association. "ACRL Diversity Alliance." Association of College & Research Libraries (ACRL), September 22, 2016. http://www.ala.org/acrl/issues/diversityalliance.

5. Jason Alston, "Causes of Satisfaction and Dissatisfaction for Diversity Resident Librarians—A Mixed Methods Study Using Herzberg's Motivation-Hygiene Theory" (Doctoral dissertation, University of South Carolina, 2017), 205, scholarcommons.sc.edu/etd/4080.

6. Sandra Hirsh et al., "Developing a Technology Integration Residency Model: The Catalyst Project Report," *Faculty Publications* (2012): 23.

7. Angela Boyd, Yolanda Blue, and Suzanne Im, "Evaluation of Academic Library Residency Programs in the United States for Librarians of Color," *College & Research Libraries* 78, no. 4 (2017): 478, doi:10.5860/crl.78.4.472.

8. Angela Galvan, "Soliciting Performance, Hiding Bias: Whiteness and Librarianship," *In the Library with the Lead Pipe*, June 3, 2015, www.inthelibrarywiththeleadpipe.org/2015/soliciting-performance-hiding-bias-whiteness-and-librarianship; April Hathcock, "White Librarianship in Blackface: Diversity Initiatives in LIS," *In the Library with the Lead Pipe*, October 7, 2015, www.inthelibrarywiththeleadpipe.org/2015/lis-diversity/; Jennifer Vinopal, "The Quest for Diversity in Library Staffing: From Awareness to Action," *In the Library with the Lead Pipe*, January 13, 2016, www.inthelibrarywiththeleadpipe.org/2016/quest-for-diversity/.

9. Martha Kyrillidou and Shaneka Morris, "ARL Annual Salary Survey 2014–2015," June 10, 2015, publications.arl.org/ARL-Annual-Salary-Survey-2014-2015/.

10. Hathcock, "White Librarianship in Blackface."

11. Ione T. Damasco and Dracine Hodges, "Tenure and Promotion Experiences of Academic Librarians of Color," *College & Research Libraries* 73, no. 3 (May 2012): 279–301.

12. Trevar Riley-Reid, "Breaking Down Barriers: Making It Easier for Academic Librarians of Color to Stay," *The Journal of Academic Librarianship* 43, no. 5 (September 1, 2017): 392–96, doi:10.1016/j.acalib.2017.06.017.

13. "Diversity Counts," *About ALA*, March 29, 2007, www.ala.org/aboutala/offices/diversity/diversitycounts/divcounts; Myrna Morales, Em Claire Knowles, and Chris Bourg, "Diversity, Social Justice, and the Future of Libraries," *Portal: Libraries and the Academy* 14, no. 3 (July 10,

2014): 439–51, doi:10.1353/pla.2014.0017; Alice H. Eagly, "Female Leadership Advantage and Disadvantage: Resolving the Contradictions," *Psychology of Women Quarterly* 31, no. 1 (2007): 1–12; Jason Martin, "Transformational and Transactional Leadership: An Exploration of Gender, Experience, and Institution Type," *Portal: Libraries and the Academy* 15, no. 2 (March 31, 2015): 331–51, doi:10.1353/pla.2015.0015.

  14. U.S. National Library of Medicine, "History of the Associate Fellowship Program," *U.S. National Library of Medicine*, August 10, 2017, www.nlm.nih.gov/about/training/associate/history.html.

  15. Margo C. Trumpeter and Paul Gherman, "A Post-Master's Degree Internship Program," *Library Journal* 105, no. 12 (June 1, 1980): 1377.

  16. Joseph A. Boissé and Connie V. Dowell, "Increasing Minority Librarians in Academic Research Libraries," *Library Journal* 112, no. 7 (1987): 52–54.

  17. Raquel V. Cogell and Cindy A. Gruwell, eds., *Diversity in Libraries: Academic Residency Programs* (Westport, Conn.: Greenwood Press, 2001).

  18. Mary Ellen Davis, "ACRL Diversity Alliance Launches," *News and Press Center*, October 11, 2016, www.ala.org/news/press-releases/2016/10/acrl-diversity-alliance-launches.

References

Alston, Jason. "Causes of Satisfaction and Dissatisfaction for Diversity Resident Librarians—A Mixed Methods Study Using Herzberg's Motivation-Hygiene Theory." Doctoral dissertation, University of South Carolina, 2017. scholarcommons.sc.edu/etd/4080.

American Library Association. "ACRL Diversity Alliance." Association of College & Research Libraries (ACRL), September 22, 2016. http://www.ala.org/acrl/issues/diversityalliance.

Association of College & Research Libraries Residency Interest Group. "FAQ—Residency Interest Group." *Residency Interest Group: An Interest Group of the Association of College & Research Libraries*, 2018. acrl.ala.org/residency/faq-2/.

Boissé, Joseph A., and Connie V. Dowell. "Increasing Minority Librarians in Academic Research Libraries." *Library Journal* 112, no. 7 (1987): 52–54.

Boyd, Angela, Yolanda Blue, and Suzanne Im. "Evaluation of Academic Library Residency Programs in the United States for Librarians of Color." *College & Research Libraries* 78, no. 4 (2017): 472–511. doi:10.5860/crl.78.4.472.

Brewer, Julie, ed. *Internship, Residency, and Fellowship Programs in ARL Libraries*. Washington, D.C.: Association of Research Libraries, Office of Management Services, 1992.

Cogell, Raquel V., and Cindy A. Gruwell, eds. *Diversity in Libraries: Academic Residency Programs*. Westport, Conn.: Greenwood Press, 2001.

Damasco, Ione T., and Dracine Hodges. "Tenure and Promotion Experiences of Academic Librarians of Color." *College & Research Libraries* 73, no. 3 (May 2012): 279–301.

Davis, Mary Ellen. "ACRL Diversity Alliance launches." *News and Press Center*, October 11, 2016. www.ala.org/news/press-releases/2016/10/acrl-diversity-alliance-launches.

"Diversity Counts." *About ALA*, March 29, 2007. www.ala.org/aboutala/offices/diversity/diversity counts/divcounts.

Eagly, Alice H. "Female Leadership Advantage and Disadvantage: Resolving the Contradictions." *Psychology of Women Quarterly* 31, no. 1 (2007): 1–12.

Galvan, Angela. "Soliciting Performance, Hiding Bias: Whiteness and Librarianship." *In the Library with the Lead Pipe*, June 3, 2015. www.inthelibrarywiththeleadpipe.org/2015/soliciting-performance-hiding-bias-whiteness-and-librarianship.

Hathcock, April. "White Librarianship in Blackface: Diversity Initiatives in LIS." *In the Library with the Lead Pipe*, October 7, 2015. www.inthelibrarywiththeleadpipe.org/2015/lis-diversity/.

Hirsh, Sandra, Ruth Metz, Scott Brown, Laura Serrano, Sheila Gurtu, Lisa Valdez, and Jane Fisher. "Developing a Technology Integration Residency Model: The Catalyst Project Report." *Faculty Publications* (2012).

Kyrillidou, Martha, and Shaneka Morris. "ARL Annual Salary Survey 2014–2015," June 10, 2015. publications.arl.org/ARL-Annual-Salary-Survey-2014-2015/.

"LA as Subject Residency Program 2018-2021." *LA as Subject*, June 8, 2016. laassubject.org/residency_program.

Martin, Jason. "Transformational and Transactional Leadership: An Exploration of Gender, Experience, and Institution Type." *Portal: Libraries and the Academy* 15, no. 2 (March 31, 2015): 331–51. doi:10.1353/pla.2015.0015.

Morales, Myrna, Em Claire Knowles, and Chris Bourg. "Diversity, Social Justice, and the Future of Libraries." *Portal: Libraries and the Academy* 14, no. 3 (July 10, 2014): 439–51. doi:10.1353/pla.2014.0017.

Riley-Reid, Trevar. "Breaking Down Barriers: Making It Easier for Academic Librarians of Color to Stay." *The Journal of Academic Librarianship* 43, no. 5 (September 1, 2017): 392–96. doi:10.1016/j.acalib.2017.06.017.

Trumpeter, Margo C., and Paul Gherman. "A Post-Master's Degree Internship Program." *Library Journal* 105, no. 12 (June 1, 1980): 1366–69.

U.S. National Library of Medicine. "History of the Associate Fellowship Program." *U.S. National Library of Medicine*, August 10, 2017. www.nlm.nih.gov/about/training/associate/history.html.

Vinopal, Jennifer. "The Quest for Diversity in Library Staffing: From Awareness to Action." *In the Library with the Lead Pipe*, January 13, 2016. www.inthelibrarywiththeleadpipe.org/2016/quest-for-diversity/.

Resources

"ACRL Residency Interest Group (RIG)." Residency Interest Group: An Interest Group of the Association of College & Research Libraries. Accessed March 9, 2018. acrl.ala.org/residency/.

Albritton, Rosie L. "Leadership Development (A CLR internship program at the University of Missouri-Columbia for recent library school graduates)." *College & Research Libraries News* (November 1987): 618–23

Alston, Jason. "Causes of Satisfaction and Dissatisfaction for Diversity Resident Librarians—A Mixed Methods Study Using Herzberg's Motivation-Hygiene Theory." Doctoral dissertation, University of South Carolina, 2017. scholarcommons.sc.edu/etd/4080.

———. "Minerva's First Born: My Experiences as UNCG's First Diversity Resident Librarian." *North Carolina Libraries* 68, no. 1 (July 19, 2010): 14. doi:10.3776/ncl.v68i1.303.

Barrie, Lita, and Rebecca Raven. "Building Our Future: The Public Library Leadership Fellows Program." *Partnership: The Canadian Journal of Library and Information Practice and Research; Toronto* 7, no. 1 (2012): 1–3.

Bello, M. A., and Y. Mansor. "Mentoring in Libraries and Information Organisation, the Catalogue Librarian Perspectives." *Library Philosophy and Practice; Lincoln* (October 2013): 1–24.

Black, William K., and Joan M. Leysen. "Fostering Success: The Socialization of Entry-Level Librarians in ARL Libraries." *Journal of Library Administration* 36, no. 4 (January 20, 2002): 3–27. doi:10.1300/J111v36n04_02.

Boissé, Joseph A., and Connie V. Dowell. "Increasing Minority Librarians in Academic Research Libraries." *Library Journal* 112, no. 7 (1987): 52–54.

Boyd, Angela, Yolanda Blue, and Suzanne Im. "Evaluation of Academic Library Residency Programs in the United States for Librarians of Color." *College & Research Libraries* 78, no. 4 (2017): 472–511. doi:10.5860/crl.78.4.472.

Brewer, Julie. "Implementing Post-Master's Residency Programs." *Leading Ideas* 4 (September 1998): 2–7.

———, ed. *Internship, Residency, and Fellowship Programs in ARL Libraries.* Washington, D.C.: Association of Research Libraries, Office of Management Services, 1992.

———. "Post-Master's Residency Programs: Enhancing the Development of New Professionals and Minority Recruitment in Academic and Research Libraries." *College & Research Libraries* 59, no. 6 (1998): 528–37. doi:10.5860/crl.59.6.528.

———. "Reflections of an Academic Library Residency Program Coordinator." In *Diversity in Libraries: Academic Residency Programs,* edited by Raquel V. Cogell and Cindy A. Gruwell, 7–16. Westport, Conn.: Greenwood Press, 2001.

———. "Understanding the Organizational Value of Post–Master's Degree Residency Programs (RLI 273, Oct. 2010)." *Research Library Issues: A Bimonthly Report from ARL, CNI, and SPARC* 272 (October 2010): 23–27. doi:10.29242/rli.272.4.

Brewer, Julie, and Mark D. Winston. "Program Evaluation for Internship/Residency Programs in Academic and Research Libraries." *College & Research Libraries* 62, no. 4 (2001): 307–15. doi:10.5860/crl.62.4.307.

Cawthorne, Jon E., and Teri B. Weil. "Internships/Residencies: Exploring the Possibilities for the Future." In *In Our Own Voices: The Changing Face of Librarianship,* edited by Teresa Neely, 45–71. Lanham, Md.: Scarecrow Press, 2003.

Cogell, Raquel V., and Cindy A. Gruwell, eds. *Diversity in Libraries: Academic Residency Programs.* Westport, Conn.: Greenwood Press, 2001.

DeBeau-Meltin, Linda, and Karen M. Beavers. "Positioning for Change: The Diversity Internship Is a Good Beginning." In *Diversity and Multiculturalism in Libraries,* edited by Katherine Hoover Hill, 227–42. Greenwich, Conn.: JAI Press, 1994.

Dewey, Barbara, and Jillian Keally. "Recruiting for Diversity: Strategies for Twenty-first Century Research Librarianship." *Library Hi Tech* 26, no. 4 (November 21, 2008): 622–29. doi:10.1108/07378830810920941.

Diaz, Jose O., and Kristina Starkus. "Increasing Minority Representation in Academic Libraries: The Minority Librarian Intern Program at the Ohio State University." *College & Research Libraries* 55, no. 1 (1994): 41–46.

Epps, Sharon K. "African American Women Leaders in Academic Research Libraries." *Portal: Libraries and the Academy* 8, no. 3 (July 18, 2008): 255–72. doi:10.1353/pla.0.0001.

Farrell, Bridget, Jaena Alabi, Pambanisha Whaley, and Claudine Jenda. "Addressing Psychosocial Factors with Library Mentoring." *Portal: Libraries and the Academy* 17, no. 1 (January 6, 2017): 51–69. doi:10.1353/pla.2017.0004.

Ghouse, Nikhat, and Jennifer Church-Duran. "And Mentoring for All: The KU Libraries' Experience." *Portal: Libraries and the Academy* 8, no. 4 (October 11, 2008): 373–86. doi:10.1353/pla.0.0022.

Goosney, Janet L., Becky Smith, and Shannon Gordon. "Reflective Peer Mentoring: Evolution of a Professional Development Program for Academic Librarians." *Partnership: The Canadian Journal of Library and Information Practice and Research* 9, no. 1 (2014). search.proquest.com/lisa/docview/1700661912/AA52D46E804B4CC7PQ/20.

"Guidelines for Practices and Principles in the Design, Operation, and Evaluation of Post-Master's Residency Programs." *Library Personnel News* 10 (May/June 1996): 1–3.

Hardesty, Larry, Mignon Adams, and Thomas G. Kirk Jr. "Nurturing a Generation of Leaders: The College Library Directors' Mentor Program." *Portal: Libraries and the Academy* 17, no. 1 (January 6, 2017): 33–49. doi:10.1353/pla.2017.0003.

Harrington, Marni R., and Elizabeth Marshall. "Analyses of Mentoring Expectations, Activities, and Support in Canadian Academic Libraries." *College & Research Libraries* 75, no. 6 (2014): 763–90. doi:10.5860/crl.75.6.763.

Henriques, Charmaine H. "Academic Research Residency Programs: Looking Back on the Journey." *Versed* (May–June 2004).

Herman, Saori Wendy. "Significant Value Found in Mentoring Programs for Novice Tenure-Track Academic Librarians." *Evidence Based Library and Information Practice; Edmonton* 11, no. 4 (2016): 91.

Hill, Katherine Hoover, ed. *Diversity and Multiculturalism in Libraries*. Greenwich, Conn.: JAI Press, 1994.

Hirsh, Sandra, Ruth Metz, Scott Brown, Laura Serrano, Sheila Gurtu, Lisa Valdez, and Jane Fisher. "Developing a Technology Integration Residency Model: The Catalyst Project Report." *Faculty Publications* (2012).

Hollis, Deborah. "On the Ambiguous Side: Experiences in a Predominantly White and Female Profession." In *In Our Own Voices: The Changing Face of Librarianship*, edited by Teresa Y. Neely and Khafre K. Abif, 139–54. Lanham, Md.: Scarecrow Press, 2003.

Hu, Sylvia. S., and Demetria E. Patrick. "Our Experience as Minority Residents: Benefits, Drawbacks, and Suggestions." *College & Research Libraries News* 67, no. 5 (2006): 297–300.

Kazmer, Michelle M. "How Do Student Experiences Differ in Online LIS Programs with and without a Residency?" *The Library Quarterly: Information, Community, Policy* 77, no. 4 (2007): 359–83. doi:10.1086/520995.

LaGuardia, Cheryl, Christine K. Oka, and Adam Griego. "Living Diversity: Making It Work." In *Diversity and Multiculturalism in Libraries*, edited by Katherine Hoover Hill, 215–26. Greenwich, Conn.: JAI Press, 1994.

Leuzinger, Julie, Jennifer Rowe, and Sian Brannon. "Mentoring Library Students for Career Development & Succession Planning." *Texas Library Journal; Houston* 92, no. 2 (Summer 2016): 46–47.

localhistorygirl. "Residency Run-down: Penn State University Libraries Diversity Residency Program." *Hiring Librarians* (blog), July 8, 2013. hiringlibrarians.com/2013/07/08/residency-run-down-penn-state-university-libraries-diversity-residency-program/.

Lorenzetti, Diane L., and Susan E. Powelson. "A Scoping Review of Mentoring Programs for Academic Librarians." *Journal of Academic Librarianship; Ann Arbor* 41, no. 2 (March 2015): 186.

Lowry, Charles B., and Paul J. Hanges. "What Is the Healthy Organization? Organizational Climate and Diversity Assessment: A Research Partnership." *Portal: Libraries and the Academy* 8, no. 1 (January 3, 2008): 1–5. doi:10.1353/pla.2008.0010.

MacKinnon, Colleen, and Susan Shepley. "Stories of Informal Mentorship: Recognizing the Voices of Mentees in Academic Libraries." *Partnership: The Canadian Journal of Library and Information Practice and Research* 9, no. 1 (April 28, 2014). doi:10.21083/partnership.v9i1.3000.

Martin, Jason. "Transformational and Transactional Leadership: An Exploration of Gender, Experience, and Institution Type." *Portal: Libraries and the Academy* 15, no. 2 (March 31, 2015): 331–51. doi:10.1353/pla.2015.0015.

Morales, Myrna, Em Claire Knowles, and Chris Bourg. "Diversity, Social Justice, and the Future of Libraries." *Portal: Libraries and the Academy* 14, no. 3 (July 10, 2014): 439–51. doi:10.1353/pla.2014.0017.

Neely, Teresa Y. "Assessing Diversity Initiatives: The ARL Leadership and Career Development Program." *Journal of Library Administration* 49, no. 8 (December 8, 2009): 811–35. doi:10.1080/01930820903396830.

Perez, Megan Z. "From New Graduate to Competent Practitioner: Rethinking the Architecture of Post-MLS Residency Programs in ARL Libraries." Master's paper, University of North Carolina, 2007. ils.unc.edu/MSpapers/3282.pdf.

Perez, Megan Zoe, and Cindy A. Gruwell. *The New Graduate Experience: Post-MLS Residency Programs and Early Career Librarianship*. Santa Barbara, Cal.: Libraries Unlimited, 2011.

Pickens, Chanelle, and Ashleigh Coren. "Diversity Residency Programs: Strategies for a Collaborative Approach to Development." *Collaborative Librarianship* 9, no. 2 (July 11, 2017). digitalcommons.du.edu/collaborativelibrarianship/vol9/iss2/7.

Raschke, Gregory K. "Hiring and Recruitment Practices in Academic Libraries: Problems and Solutions." *Portal: Libraries and the Academy* 3, no. 1 (February 5, 2003): 53–67. doi:10.1353/pla.2003.0017.

Reese, Gregory L., and Ernestine L. Hawkins. *Stop Talking, Start Doing!: Attracting People of Color to the Library Profession.* Chicago: American Library Association, 1999.

Ross, Kevin M. "Purposeful Mentoring in Academic Libraries." *Journal of Library Administration* 53, no. 7–8 (2013): 412–28. doi:10.1080/01930826.2013.882195.

Sapon-White, Richard, Valery King, and Anne Christie. "Supporting a Culture of Scholarship for Academic Librarians." *Portal: Libraries and the Academy* 4, no. 3 (July 9, 2004): 407–21. doi:10.1353/pla.2004.0044.

Saylor, Nicole, Jen Wolfe, and Paul Soderdahl. "Mentoring, It's a Good Thing: What We Learned Partying with Student Librarians." *College & Research Libraries News* 72, no. 10 (2011): 566–70.

Scherrer, Carol S. "Evaluating a Health Sciences Library Residency Program: What Have We Learned?" *Journal of the Medical Library Association* 98 (October 2, 2010): 1–4. doi:10.3163/1536-5050.98.4.006.

Seal, Robert A. "The Merits of Mentoring." *Portal: Libraries and the Academy* 15, no. 4 (October 6, 2015): 565–69.

Sears, Suzanne. "Mentoring to Grow Library Leaders." *Journal of Library Administration* 54, no. 2 (February 17, 2014): 127–34. doi:10.1080/01930826.2014.903368.

Smith, Felicia A. "Reflections of a Resident." *Versed* (September–October 2005).

Smith, Paula M. "Culturally Conscious Organizations: A Conceptual Framework." *Portal: Libraries and the Academy* 8, no. 2 (April 4, 2008): 141–55. doi:10.1353/pla.2008.0015.

Switzer, T., and W. Gentz. "Increasing Diversity: Programs and Internships in ARL Libraries." *Advances in Librarianship* 23 (1999): 169–88.

Tewell, Eamon C. "Employment Opportunities for New Academic Librarians: Assessing the Availability of Entry Level Jobs." *Portal: Libraries and the Academy* 12, no. 4 (October 4, 2012): 407–23.

Triumph, Therese F., and Penny M. Beile. "The Trending Academic Library Job Market: An Analysis of Library Position Announcements from 2011 with Comparisons to 1996 and 1988." *College & Research Libraries* 76, no. 6 (2015). doi:10.5860/crl.76.6.716.

Trumpeter, Margo C., and Paul Gherman. "A Post-Master's Degree Internship Program." *Library Journal* 105, no. 12 (June 1, 1980): 1366–69.

Velez, Cecilia P. "Academic Libraries Meeting the Challenge of Affirmative Action: The University of California at Santa Barbara Experience." *Reforma Newsletter* (Summer 1989): 11, 15.

Welburn, William C. "Creating Inclusive Communities: Diversity and the Responses of Academic Libraries." *Portal: Libraries and the Academy* 10, no. 3 (July 10, 2010): 355–63. doi:10.1353/pla.0.0107.

CHAPTER 2

Why Should My Library Consider Hosting a Residency Program?

HOSTING A RESIDENCY PROGRAM is a big decision for any library: It is a big monetary commitment and a big time commitment. There are human resources, space, and training commitments that must be made. However, for institutions that are willing and able to commit these resources, developing a residency provides benefits to the institution, its stakeholders, and the resident. Because establishing, implementing, maintaining, and continuously improving residency programs requires such steep time, energy, and effort commitments, libraries interested in establishing or re-establishing residency programs should have honest internal conversations as to why they are interested in hosting a residency program. Potential host libraries also need to consider the benefits of establishing residency programs. Those exploring hosting a residency should consider the benefits of establishing residency programs as well as the challenges; this chapter will focus largely on the benefits of establishing a residency program.

Benefits to the Librarian Profession

Hosting a residency program offers benefits that go beyond the walls of the host library. While it is not uncommon for residents to remain with the host institution in some capacity after the residency term ends, most resident librarians move on to other institutions to continue their careers. Therefore, your library's residency program has the potential to help libraries far and wide. A successful residency program provides the entire profession with highly skilled talent.

Retaining Second-Career Librarians

Residencies can play a role in helping candidates who are transitioning into librarianship. Given the interdisciplinary nature of library and information science, librarians possessing experience in other career fields can greatly benefit the library profession. Residency programs give these candidates realistic opportunities to gain entry-level employment and learn the vital library-specific skills that will be useful when looking for permanent positions in libraries. Residencies are not the only opportunities for those who transition into libraries from other fields to find employment but still prove to be a useful tool in this regard; in his dissertation, Jason Alston interviewed eleven current and former resident librarians for a qualitative portion of his research, of which at least three had transitioned into libraries from other career fields through a residency program.[1]

Retaining Diverse Residents

Diversity residencies specifically are a key method by which the library profession as a whole can build the presence of librarians from underrepresented groups. North American libraries have long struggled to diversify, particularly in the area of race and ethnicity of practitioners. According to the most recent "Diversity Counts" figures released by the American Library Association in 2012, about 88 percent of the professional librarian workforce in America is non-Hispanic white,[2] while only about 60 percent of the general U.S. population is non-Hispanic white according to 2017 estimates from the U.S. Census Bureau.[3] The American Library Association's figures from 1990 reflect that the American librarian workforce was 88 percent non-Hispanic white at that time as well, suggesting that the field is not keeping pace with the increasing racial and ethnic diversity of the U.S. population at large[4]; the general population of the United States of America was 76 percent non-Hispanic white in 1990.[5] Diversity residencies can provide candidates from diverse backgrounds the opportunity for professional development and growth and can contribute to the capacity of the whole library profession to reflect and serve its many communities. In addition, residencies give early-career librarians from underrepresented groups an opportunity to have a positive experience in the profession, which will hopefully encourage them to persist in librarianship.

Julie Brewer of the University of Delaware notes that residency programs can also enable early-career librarians to gain the job experience they need to be able to contribute immediately to their libraries. According to Brewer, "The professional staff in large research libraries is typically dominated by mid-career and late-career librarians."[6] Many libraries may not be able to find a need for candidates fresh out of library school who have practically no professional librarian experience. However, residencies afford early-career librarians a chance to learn skills quickly and then move on to libraries that can make use of the newly developed skill set and incorporate an early-career librarian into a professional culture where mid-career and late-career librarians dominate. Multigenerational workplaces in general, not just libraries, can thrive because of the variation of ideas, wisdom, and knowledge among the staff; competencies with customers of various ages and technologies of various forms also strengthen multigenerational workplaces.[7]

⊚ Benefits for Your Library

Potential Infusion of New Energy

There are a number of studies that suggest that engaged employees tend to be more productive and effective than employees that are disengaged.[8] This is not a groundbreaking revelation by any means, but the evidence that engaged employees perform better is reason enough to make sure that the employees at a particular library maintain a palpable level of motivation. Although employee energy is becoming increasingly depleted in current work climates due to such factors as longer and more intense work hours, "relational energy" wherein workers derive energy from relationships with coworkers on the job may offset burnout.[9] As new librarians, many residents contribute perspectives that have not yet been considered to their host institutions' organizational cultures, which can invigorate existing work with positive energy. This positive energy could be a resource for other employees struggling with burnout or disengagement.[10] Hosting organizations should be cautious, though, as toxic organizational cultures can negatively impact the resident. While residents can bring fresh, positive energy into a library, they are new professionals and therefore should not be expected to work alone as change agents.[11]

Potential Infusion of Fresh Ideas

Thura Mack, a residency coordinator and supervisor with the University of Tennessee–Knoxville, has supervised resident librarians since 2003. Mack insists that with each cycle of residents, the libraries at UTK benefit from the residents' unique perspectives and approaches. These unique ideas and perspectives can spring from various factors. For instance, Mack says that diversity residents may choose to guide improvement of practices and processes at a university library to make them more inclusive because these residents bring with them the perspectives of those who come from traditionally disenfranchised or underrepresented populations. Residents who worked as paraprofessionals at other institutions prior to earning their library science degree may also come in with ideas that they developed at their previous jobs, and Mack says that these ideas can be merged with existing practices at an institution to improve procedures and workflows. Also, just as those coming into librarianship from other career fields can benefit the profession at large with the skill sets that they are bringing in from these other professions, such residents will also be able to lean on those skill sets to devise new ideas that aid the host institution. However, it is important to remember that residents, especially those from underrepresented groups, should not be required or expected to participate in diversity initiatives or use skills from their past professions unless they express an interest in doing so. Residents, as short-term new professionals, are vulnerable at institutions, and requiring them to take on the work of managing diversity initiatives increases this vulnerability.

Increased Communication and Collaboration Between Departments

Currently, about one out of three residency programs focuses their residents solely within one department of the academic library, but most residencies either rotate the resident through various library departments or find other ways to have the resident gain work experience outside of any primarily assigned department. If the resident librarian rotates through different departments, hosting a residency affords the host institution an opportunity for increased and enhanced interdepartmental communication and collaboration. When planning a residency that gives the resident hands-on experience with multiple departments, library personnel from various departments will have to come together in order to assemble a residency plan of action that makes optimal use of the resident's limited amount of time with any departments involved. This planning can allow library personnel from varying departments to learn in more detail about the responsibilities and core competencies of staff in other departments; this exposure can lead to a better understanding of the roles of other departments in the library. The residency can also serve as an initiative in which traditionally compartmentalized departments within an academic library have an opportunity to interrupt traditional siloing. Rather, these units should behave as vital organs within an entire body that must function together for the initiative to be successful. Planned and implemented appropriately, a residency program can actively contribute to a healthier organizational culture across a whole academic library.

Breaking Down Institutional Inertia

In a 2016 monograph, former resident librarian Jason Alston surveyed former diversity residents in an informal study.[12] Feedback from the participating former residents suggested that while those serving as the first resident or in the first residency cohort at their institution may have faced institutional hostilities and resistance toward the residency concept, those who served after the first resident or first cohort of residents may have had better experiences at the same institutions. If objection to and resistance toward residency programs does indeed dwindle across cycles at some libraries, then this indicates that over time, attitudes within the organizational culture at these host institutions are evolving and forsaking previous resistance to change and the implementation of new initiatives. In the library field, a dynamic institution is better equipped to serve patrons in a country with rapidly changing demographics and technological habits than an institution that attempts to remain static and not implement new initiatives.

Libraries that commit to implementing residency programs and then continue to assess and improve their residencies despite initial difficulties will prove to internal and external observers that they have the ability to adapt and potentially even embrace change. These libraries may then attract more workers that are interested in working for dynamic institutions. Also, workers at such libraries may feel more positively toward change initiatives; workers who are in a culture where organizational change is managed well may become acclimated to such change. A residency program may therefore fit into a larger paradigm of change being accepted and embraced at a progressive library.

Support for Unique Projects

Although many residents contribute to ongoing library initiatives during their tenure at an institution, having a resident also offers the opportunity to have a librarian work on a short-term specialized project as well. After being employed with an institution for some time, permanent employees may find themselves committed to a variety of responsibilities within the host institution that leave them little time to integrate new projects into their workflow. Some such projects may be best suited for a resident librarian to take the lead on, particularly if that resident approaches the project from the mindset of completing it within the residency term. In many cases, residents will also have cutting-edge knowledge or best practices about how to approach the project.

Julie Brewer, who has served as a residency coordinator for the University of Delaware, explains that attempting to investigate new trends and service possibilities with traditional staff would often require either a request for new positions or reassigning the duties of existing personnel. The duties of residents, Brewer contends, are potentially more flexible.[13] Using residents in these more temporary or investigative roles prevents the interruption of long-standing workflows.

Librarians Janet L. Mayo and Angela P. Whitehurst of East Carolina University note that "little published material about the use of temporary librarians in higher education seems to exist"[14] and described several advantages that hiring term-limited librarians may potentially provide an academic library. Through a survey of fourteen academic library administrators, Mayo and Whitehurst find that most of the participants responded that they appreciated the "flexibility and specific focus" that hiring term-limited librarians can afford them.[15] Residents, like other term-limited librarians, can tackle projects that are particularly suited to their skill sets and can be completed within the residency term. However, this flexibility should not come at the expense of funding permanent jobs when possible. Please review chapter 8 for further discussion.

Networking

As will be discussed later in this chapter, residency programs afford the resident the chance to network with other professionals. However, residency programs also afford the hosting institution with increased networking opportunities. Hosting institutions can take advantage of the opportunity to establish connections with other hosting institutions through such avenues as ACRL's Diversity Alliance or simply create local networks with institutions that either host residencies or are considering hosting residencies. Librarian Thura Mack encourages host institutions to reach out to one another and share best practices. According to Mack, institutions that host residencies are positioned for a perfect opportunity to work together and establish fruitful relationships "because we want to help each other, [and] we all want all of the programs to succeed."

Mack attributes the residency to providing her with opportunities to publish and present, not just due to her personal experience coordinating and supervising UTK's own program but also due to collaborating and sharing ideas with residency coordinators and supervisors at other institutions. In the spirit of Mack's testimony, host institutions can take solace in the idea that while there may be competition between programs for the best potential residents to hire, once residents are placed, the pool of hosting programs tends to be cooperative with one another, not hostile or competitive with each other. If hosting institutions are working toward similar goals, communication with librarians from other hosting institutions can improve practice across the board.

Enhancement of the Library's Reputation Within the Field

Residency programs can also draw attention to the libraries that host them, enhancing the library's reputation to potential employees and other interested parties. Those libraries that manage to host successful residency programs, especially over the course of multiple cycles, are often thought to be well-functioning libraries that are good places to work. Libraries can therefore enhance their attractiveness to potential employees by successfully hosting a residency program. This can be especially beneficial for libraries in states that do not have accredited library science programs and do not often serve as sites for library conferences. The activities of libraries in these states may not be as well-known as libraries in states that often host conferences and benefit from the presence of accredited library school programs. However, these schools have the ability to use their library websites and other venues to publicize the success of their residency programs, and potential applicants who may have otherwise been hesitant to apply for jobs at these libraries could potentially feel more comfortable doing so.

Benefits for Residency Coordinators and Supervisors

Residency coordinators and supervisors can also benefit from participating in residencies. Duties such as serving on the residency search committee, supporting and supervising residents, and participating in other elements of the program can provide opportunities to develop new skills. Many librarian jobs beyond the entry level seek candidates that have supervisory and/or management experience. Librarians who have exceeded the entry ranks often have to supervise entry-level librarians, paraprofessionals including library specialists, student workers, volunteers, and others. Librarians who aspire to become department heads or library administrators can strengthen their case for being hired into these positions by demonstrating a history of project management experience. A residency cycle functions like a project cycle, and supervisors and coordinators who administer a residency from the beginning to the end of a cycle can make the case that they have successfully managed a library project or initiative to its cyclical conclusion.

Personal Fulfillment

Residency coordinators may glean personal satisfaction and fulfillment from being involved with guiding, mentoring, and nurturing residents who later go on to be successful in librarianship. Thura Mack says that her role as a residency coordinator "has definitely been one of the highlights of my career" and says she truly feels that she has established ongoing bonds with her previous residents that go beyond just being professional contacts. Gerald Holmes, who was involved in planning and coordinating a diversity residency program at the University of North Carolina at Greensboro, also says that he takes personal fulfillment from working on and coordinating residencies and that he enjoys following the careers and learning about the accomplishments of residency alumni who had come through UNCG's program.

Potential Service Opportunity for Academic Librarians

Academic librarians must often have some mixture of scholarship, teaching/practice, and service recorded in their professional activity to receive tenure, promotion, or reappointment. These requirements vary from institution to institution. What will count as scholarship, teaching/practice, and service will also vary depending on the institution. Coordinating or supervising a residency cycle may count as practice, or it may count as service. This will depend on the institution, and supervisors/coordinators are advised to check with library administrators to determine which category of professional activity their role with the residency will count toward. However, there is a chance that taking on this role will demonstrate commitment to these requirements of academic librarianship when going for promotion, tenure, or reappointment and that you can perform effectively at achieving the goals and objectives laid out by previous annual reviews.

⑥ Benefits for the Resident

If the residency program is planned and implemented properly, the librarians who partic-ipate will benefit greatly from the program. In general, resident librarians will gain practi-cal skills and knowledge during the residency beyond what they acquired while working on their master's degrees in library and information science. Hosting libraries must take care, however, to ensure that the work of a resident goes beyond what is expected of a graduate student intern. Therefore, when crafting a residency program, take some care to ensure that residents are able to do work that benefits their future careers.

A First Professional Librarian Job

In many career fields, one does not have to search long before finding a lot of recent graduates bemoaning the current state of the job market and complaining that so many advertised positions require professional experience for consideration. The library field is no different in this regard. While some library school programs, such as the iSchool at the University of Illinois, have recently reported record or otherwise growing enrollments,[16] the long-touted "massive retirement wave" predicted to hit the librarian field still has not yet happened, with 2017 seeing yet another claim of an impending retirement wave.[17] The frustration of newly minted librarians not having enough professional experience to land their first library job is strong enough that former INALJ Georgia head editor Courtney Baron has advised library school students and recent graduates that an internship or other kind of experience is required to get even an entry-level position.[18]

It is not easy for many new library school graduates to land their first professional librarian job. Those recruited into library schools but who lack previous library experience, be it as library paraprofessionals, student workers, volunteers, or otherwise, may face a particularly uphill battle when attempting to compete against those who enrolled in library school after having served in one of these aforementioned roles. Such new grad-uates who lack practical library work experience often still have much to offer the library profession, particularly if they are transitioning from other professions and are aware of how their skill set can aid them in being effective librarians. However, due to their lack of experience, these new graduates who possess amazing potential may find requirements for two to three years of library experience too steep a criterion to overcome.

Residency programs, which often target recent library school graduates with no post-master's experience, can be a useful tool in alleviating this obstacle for newly grad-uated librarians. A resident librarian should go into this first professional appointment with an understanding that the residency is a time-limited appointment but that the typical duration of two to three years will match the required minimum professional experience in many librarian job postings.

Enhanced Job Prospects

Adjacent to the ever-important first professional job, residents can also benefit from enhanced job prospects once they complete their residencies. Several factors contribute to this. First and foremost is experience, as those who complete a residency program will usually have one to three years of professional librarian experience. As most residency programs are open to those with no professional librarian experience, this means that the same librarian who had no professional librarian experience prior to completing the residency now has the one to three years of experience that is often listed in many professional librarian job ads.

In addition to the experience, residents also may have a chance to earn a permanent position with the host institution. While most residencies do not guarantee that a resident will be able to stay on with the host institution once the residency term ends, it is not unheard of for institutions to hire their own program alumni for permanent positions after the residency term has ended.

Filling Potential Knowledge/Skills Gaps

At least as far back as 1983, librarians have expressed that some gaps exist between the skills and knowledge with which library school graduates are completing programs and what skills and knowledge these libraries need their practitioners to have.[19] Discussions in the early 1980s to remedy this involved the idea of expanding the curricula of MLS programs. However, many disadvantages to the idea of expanding library school curricula were advanced during that time. Former University of South Carolina School of Library Science dean William Summers suggested that to do so would not lead to substantive change but rather "at heart a decision to do more of the same."[20] Other criticisms of the idea of expanding programs included the increased cost to complete a degree and what effect expanded curricula would have on students who were only able to attend graduate school part time.

In 1983, the University of Michigan published an article in *Library Journal* detailing its plan to move forward with establishing a "research library residency." Justification for establishing a residency program included that such a move could equip the resident with skills and a knowledge base that they were not able to obtain solely from library school education or internship. For instance, in chapter 5, Alexandra Provo, a former resident, notes that her residency program provided her with knowledge she wished she might have received in an internship. Library science education has remained under scrutiny in more recent times, with such critiques as library school programs being "diploma mills,"[21] not instilling an adequate amount of "soft skills" in students,[22] not achieving a proper balance of theory and practice within instruction,[23] and failing to offer coursework in key areas of librarianship such as data curation[24] and access services.[25] Residency programs give new professionals the opportunity to acquire knowledge and skill sets, with pay and without tuition fees, that they either could not or did not gain during their library school education. If a residency is rotation-based, there is also an enhanced chance that the resident will have the opportunity to explore how workflows, systems, and processes work in other library departments. Understanding these various systems may help the resident better understand and appreciate the job functions of coworkers in other departments for the duration of their career.

Discovering Professional Interests

Programs that rotate residents throughout differing departments or otherwise afford the resident opportunities to get on-the-job work experience in multiple departments provide opportunities for new librarians to explore work and research interests. Former resident librarian Quetzalli Barrientos notes that her residency program afforded additional opportunities to discover her interests and passions within librarianship.[26] Residency programs mostly employ degreed librarians who have little to no post-master's experience. Residents may therefore not yet know on which area(s) of librarianship they wish to focus their careers. Even if a resident has previous library experience as a paraprofessional, student worker, page, or volunteer, these forms of practical library experience often charge the worker/volunteer with a specific duty in the library and might not afford the worker/volunteer with much exposure to functions outside of the regularly assigned tasks. Therefore, even residents who have previous experience working in libraries in one of these capacities may not truly know for which area of librarianship they are best suited.

Librarians who discover and are subsequently empowered to work in the area of librarianship that is best suited for them are more likely to remain in the field of librarianship. Residency coordinators should take care to give residents some guidance on exploring their possibilities within the library field and ensure that residents have access to mentorship on this from other experienced librarians.[27]

Unique Opportunities to Build a Professional Network Early

Residency programs often give residents professional development funding in order to accelerate the resident's preparedness for the open job market. Some residents may receive more professional development funding than other positions do and thus may have the opportunity to attend more conferences and workshops during their residency terms than other library employees. Because of this, a savvy resident librarian is placed in a strong position where they can enhance their professional network before landing their first permanent position. Residents also have the opportunity to establish long-lasting connections with coworkers and other colleagues at the host institution before moving on. Also, as Barrientos notes, residents are able to network with one another and with former residents through such avenues as the Association of College and Research Library's (ACRL) Residency Interest Group.[28]

Opportunities to Learn About Academia and Higher Education

There are some entities in the field of library and information science that are not academic libraries but have hosted residency programs, such as the Online Computer Library Center (OCLC), the National Library of Medicine, and Los Angeles Public Library. The majority of library residency programs, however, have been hosted at academic libraries. Barrientos posits that those who serve in residency programs at academic libraries not only have the opportunity to learn more about librarianship while serving as residents but may also get a chance to learn more about academia.[29] Residents in academic libraries should have the opportunity to learn about the promotion and tenure processes both within and outside of the library at the hosting college or university. If residents have visiting faculty status, this may afford them chances to attend or perhaps even be involved with the faculty senate. Residents who are given liaison duties with any departments or organizations on campus may have opportunities to do things like attend departmental/organizational meetings or be added to listservs; following departmental or organizational communications can help a resident understand how these campus entities function. Also, actual practice can help residents reinforce their grasp on concepts that they likely already had some familiarity with from their collegiate and graduate school studies; for instance, residents may already have a firm grasp on the difference between scholarly and nonscholarly sources due to their graduate studies, but having to understand these differences when assisting students or doing their own research may fortify their understanding of the distinction.

Be aware of all of these benefits when making the case to begin or continue a residency program. Some faculty and staff at any host institution or potential host institution may not support the idea of hosting a residency. Courting buy-in and support for the residency is helpful in making it successful, particularly from the standpoint of the residents.[30] While it is unrealistic to expect that all personnel will embrace and offer support for the program, being able to explain the benefits of hosting a program could garner support and buy-in for the residency initiative.

⑥ Key Points

- Residency programs can benefit the profession by helping early-career librarians who are recent graduates or entering librarianship from another career learn on-the-job skills.
- Diversity residencies in particular are an important strategy to diversify the profession.
- Residency programs offer benefits to coordinators, supervisors, and residents, including the chance to learn and practice new skills.

⑥ Notes

1. Jason Alston, "Causes of Satisfaction and Dissatisfaction for Diversity Resident Librarians—A Mixed Methods Study Using Herzberg's Motivation-Hygiene Theory" (Doctoral dissertation, University of South Carolina, 2017), /scholarcommons.sc.edu/etd/4080.

2. "Diversity Counts," *About ALA* (March 29, 2007), www.ala.org/aboutala/offices/diversity/diversitycounts/divcounts.

3. U.S. Census Bureau, "U.S. Census Bureau QuickFacts: UNITED STATES," accessed November 12, 2018, www.census.gov/quickfacts/fact/table/US/PST045217.

4. Thomas Godfrey and Stephen J. Tordella, *Librarians, Library Technicians and Assistants: Diversity Profile 2000 and 1990, Library Employees Living in Same Sex Partner Households, First Look from the American Community Survey* (Arlington, Va.: Decision Demographics, May 10, 2006).

5. Campbell Gibson and Kay Jung, "Historical Census Statistics on Population Totals by Race, 1790 to 1990, and by Hispanic Origin, 1790 to 1990, for the United States, Regions, Divisions, and States" (Washington, D.C.: US Census Bureau, 2002).

6. Julie Brewer, "Understanding the Organizational Value of Post–Master's Degree Residency Programs (RLI 273, Oct. 2010)," *Research Library Issues: A Bimonthly Report from ARL, CNI, and SPARC* 272 (October 2010): 24, doi:10.29242/rli.272.4.

7. Wes Gay, "Why a Multigenerational Workforce Is a Competitive Advantage," *Forbes*, October 20, 2017, www.forbes.com/sites/wesgay/2017/10/20/multigeneration-workforce/.

8. Bruce Louis Rich, Jeffrey A. Lepine, and Eean R. Crawford, "Job Engagement: Antecedents and Effects on Job Performance," *Academy of Management Journal* 53, no. 3 (2010): 617–35.

9. Bradley P. Owens et al., "Relational Energy at Work: Implications for Job Engagement and Job Performance," *Journal of Applied Psychology* 101, no. 1 (2016): 35.

10. Wilmar B. Schaufeli and Arnold B. Bakker, "Job Demands, Job Resources, and Their Relationship with Burnout and Engagement: A Multi-Sample Study," *Journal of Organizational Behavior: The International Journal of Industrial, Occupational and Organizational Psychology and Behavior* 25, no. 3 (2004): 293–315.

11. Alston, "Causes of Satisfaction and Dissatisfaction," 139–40.

12. Jason Alston, "Interns or Professionals? A Common Misnomer Applied to Diversity Resident Librarians Can Potentially Degrade and Divide," in *Where Are All the Librarians of Color?: The Experiences of People of Color in Academia*, ed. Rebecca Hankins and Miguel Juárez (San Francisco, Cal.: Library Juice Press, 2015).

13. Julie Brewer, "Understanding the Organizational Value."

14. Janet L. Mayo and Angela P. Whitehurst, "Temporary Librarians in Academe: Current Use, Future Considerations," *Reference Services Review* 40, no. 3 (2012): 513.

15. Ibid., 519.

16. University of Illinois Urbana-Champaign, School of Information Sciences, "iSchool Experiences Record Enrollment," *School of Information Sciences*, December 7, 2017, ischool.illinois.edu/news-events/news/2017/12/ischool-experiences-record-enrollment.

17. Phil Davis, "Retirement Wave To Hit Academic Librarianship," *The Scholarly Kitchen*, October 19, 2017, scholarlykitchen.sspnet.org/2017/10/19/retirement-wave-hit-librarianship/.

18. Courtney Baron, "3 Ways to Get Library Experience without a Library Job," *INALJ*, September 23, 2014, inalj.com/?p=23768.

19. Richard M. Dougherty and Wendy P. Lougee, "Research Library Residencies: A New Model for Professional Development," *Library Journal* 108, no. 13 (1983): 1322–24.

20. Ibid.,1323.

21. Annoyed Librarian, "Consider the Poor LIS Professors," *Library Journal*, September 5, 2017, lj.libraryjournal.com/blogs/annoyedlibrarian/2017/09/05/consider-the-poor-lis-professors/. The pseudonymous columnist is responding to the labeling of library schools as diploma mills by someone in the comments section of a previous column.

22. Emma J. Cobb, Jennifer Meixelsperger, and Kadie K. Seitz, "Beyond the Classroom: Fostering Soft Skills in Pre-Professional LIS Organizations," *Journal of Library Administration* 55, no. 2 (2015): 114–20.

23. Carla J. Stoffle and Kim Leeder, "Practitioners and Library Education: A Crisis of Understanding," *Journal of Education for Library and Information Science* 46, no. 4 (2005): 312–19.

24. Rebecca L. Harris-Pierce and Yan Quan Liu, "Is Data Curation Education at Library and Information Science Schools in North America Adequate?" *New Library World* 113, no. 11/12 (2012): 598–613.

25. David McCaslin, "Access Services Education in Library and Information Science Programs," *Journal of Access Services* 6, no. 4 (2009): 485–96.

26. Quetzalli Barrientos, "Library Residency Programs: The Pros and Cons of Residency Positions as Written by a Current Resident," *ACRLog*, October 24, 2016, acrlog.org/2016/10/24/library-residency-programs-the-pros-and-cons-of-residency-positions-as-written-by-a-current-resident/.

27. Alston, "Causes of Satisfaction and Dissatisfaction."

28. Barrientos, "Library Residency Programs."

29. Ibid.

30. Alston, "Causes of Satisfaction and Dissatisfaction."

⑥ References

Alston, Jason. "Causes of Satisfaction and Dissatisfaction for Diversity Resident Librarians—A Mixed Methods Study Using Herzberg's Motivation-Hygiene Theory." Doctoral dissertation, University of South Carolina, 2017. scholarcommons.sc.edu/etd/4080.

———. "Interns or Professionals? A Common Misnomer Applied to Diversity Resident Librarians Can Potentially Degrade and Divide." In *Where Are All the Librarians of Color?: The Experiences of People of Color in Academia*, edited by Rebecca Hankins and Miguel Juárez. San Francisco, Cal.: Library Juice Press, 2015.

Annoyed Librarian. "Consider the Poor LIS Professors." *Library Journal*, September 5, 2017. lj.libraryjournal.com/blogs/annoyedlibrarian/2017/09/05/consider-the-poor-lis-professors/.

Baron, Courtney. "3 Ways to Get Library Experience without a Library Job." *INALJ*, September 23, 2014. inalj.com/?p=23768.

Barrientos, Quetzalli. "Library Residency Programs: The Pros and Cons of Residency Positions as Written by a Current Resident." *ACRLog*, October 24, 2016. acrlog.org/2016/10/24/library-residency-programs-the-pros-and-cons-of-residency-positions-as-written-by-a-current-resident/.

Brewer, Julie. "Understanding the Organizational Value of Post–Master's Degree Residency Programs (RLI 273, Oct. 2010)." *Research Library Issues: A Bimonthly Report from ARL, CNI, and SPARC* 272 (October 2010): 23–27. doi:10.29242/rli.272.4.

Cobb, Emma J., Jennifer Meixelsperger, and Kadie K. Seitz. "Beyond the Classroom: Fostering Soft Skills in Pre-Professional LIS Organizations." *Journal of Library Administration* 55, no. 2 (2015): 114–20.

Davis, Phil. "Retirement Wave To Hit Academic Librarianship." *The Scholarly Kitchen*, October 19, 2017. scholarlykitchen.sspnet.org/2017/10/19/retirement-wave-hit-librarianship/.

"Diversity Counts." *About ALA*, March 29, 2007. www.ala.org/aboutala/offices/diversity/diversity counts/divcounts.

Dougherty, Richard M., and Wendy P. Lougee. "Research Library Residencies: A New Model for Professional Development." *Library Journal* 108, no. 13 (1983): 1322–24.

Gay, Wes. "Why a Multigenerational Workforce Is a Competitive Advantage." *Forbes*, October 20, 2017. www.forbes.com/sites/wesgay/2017/10/20/multigeneration-workforce/.

Gibson, Campbell, and Kay Jung. "Historical Census Statistics on Population Totals by Race, 1790 to 1990, and by Hispanic Origin, 1790 to 1990, for the United States, Regions, Divisions, and States." Washington, D.C.: U.S. Census Bureau, 2002.

Godfrey, Thomas, and Stephen J. Tordella. *Librarians, Library Technicians and Assistants: Diversity Profile 2000 and 1990, Library Employees Living in Same Sex Partner Households, First Look from the American Community Survey*. Arlington, Va.: Decision Demographics, May 10, 2006.

Harris-Pierce, Rebecca L., and Yan Quan Liu. "Is Data Curation Education at Library and Information Science Schools in North America Adequate?" *New Library World* 113, no. 11/12 (2012): 598–613.

Mayo, Janet L., and Angela P. Whitehurst. "Temporary Librarians in Academe: Current Use, Future Considerations." *Reference Services Review* 40, no. 3 (2012): 512–24.

McCaslin, David. "Access Services Education in Library and Information Science Programs." *Journal of Access Services* 6, no. 4 (2009): 485–96.

Owens, Bradley P., Wayne E. Baker, Dana McDaniel Sumpter, and Kim S. Cameron. "Relational Energy at Work: Implications for Job Engagement and Job Performance." *Journal of Applied Psychology* 101, no. 1 (2016): 35.

Rich, Bruce Louis, Jeffrey A. Lepine, and Eean R. Crawford. "Job Engagement: Antecedents and Effects on Job Performance." *Academy of Management Journal* 53, no. 3 (2010): 617–35.

Schaufeli, Wilmar B., and Arnold B. Bakker. "Job Demands, Job Resources, and Their Relationship with Burnout and Engagement: A Multi-Sample Study." *Journal of Organizational Behavior: The International Journal of Industrial, Occupational and Organizational Psychology and Behavior* 25, no. 3 (2004): 293–315.

Stoffle, Carla J., and Kim Leeder. "Practitioners and Library Education: A Crisis of Understanding." *Journal of Education for Library and Information Science* 46, no. 4 (2005): 312–19.

University of Illinois Urbana-Champaign, School of Information Sciences. "iSchool Experiences Record Enrollment." *School of Information Sciences*, December 7, 2017. ischool.illinois.edu/news-events/news/2017/12/ischool-experiences-record-enrollment.

U.S. Census Bureau. "U.S. Census Bureau QuickFacts: UNITED STATES." Accessed November 12, 2018. www.census.gov/quickfacts/fact/table/US/PST045217.

Developing Support for a Residency Program

WHEN AN INSTITUTION FIRST CONSIDERS hosting a library residency program, it can be tempting to jump in and get things started right away. However, rushing the process of developing support for the residency often leads to problems down the line. Instead, take time to make sure that the program will thrive at the host institution and that all of the appropriate stakeholders are on board. In particular, gaining support from administrators to commit the needed funds and other resources to make the program successful is crucial. This chapter offers practical ideas for how to build support for the residency, including how to identify key stakeholders, gain administrative support by aligning the residency goals with library and university goals, and communicate the purpose of the residency effectively.

Review and Gather Information About Residencies

Review this book and other resources to make sure you are familiar with the basics of residencies. Contact peer institutions with residency programs and communicate with members of the ACRL Residency Interest Group or a similar group to get a sense of how other libraries have negotiated the challenges of creating and maintaining a residency.

These institutions may be able to provide you with a sense of their timeline for developing their program, the steps they took to promote and develop it, and any positive outcomes for the institution or prior participants. Getting some information about others doing a similar program can save you from having to reinvent the wheel.

Identify Stakeholders

Stakeholders are defined as "any group or individual who can affect or is affected by the achievement of a corporation's purpose."[1] When it comes to library residencies, stakeholders include any person or group whose support is required to make the program a success or who will be affected by the program. Although some stakeholders will be direct players and interact with the resident, even peripheral stakeholders like friends of the library groups can contribute to and advertise the program. Stakeholders can both detract from or encourage a residency program's success, so discussing the goals of the program with stakeholders is essential.[2]

In a residency program, obvious stakeholders would be administrators who provide resources, but there are often many other stakeholders as well, such as peers whose work lives will be changed by interacting with the resident, departments that will be required to train and support the resident during rotations, and Friends of the Library or advisory boards that will need to support the program. Take some time to figure out who the stakeholders for a project are, what their role in the project might be, what resources they can contribute, what they want out of the program, and what questions or concerns they may have.[3]

Table 3.1. Sample List of Stakeholders to Consider When Planning a Residency Program

STAKEHOLDER	ROLE IN PROJECT	RESOURCES	GOALS	QUESTIONS AND CONCERNS
Dean	Sponsor	Funding, support for project	Positive exposure for the library Increased retention of librarians	What is the cost of this project? Will this divert necessary resources from another part of the library? How will campus administration react to this proposal?
Associate Dean	Sponsor	Funding, training resources	Positive outcomes for departments in division Reductions of projects in the backlog	What kinds of projects could the resident work on? How will this project affect my division's access to resources?
Department Head	Manager	Training support, possibly management	Positive outcome for department	Who will work with this person in my department? How can we manage the resident's work flow effectively?
Diversity and Inclusion Committee	Hiring committee	Time for hiring process, advocacy	Supporting diversity initiatives in the library and profession	What role can we play in integrating this person into other campus and library initiatives? How should we hire?

Developing a Persuasive Project Proposal

After identifying stakeholders, the next step is to create a strong proposal that articulates the benefits of a residency for the institution while laying out the resources, skills, and relationships necessary to make the program a success. One helpful way to develop a proposal is to look at how fund raisers plan for and request funds from donors, a process called "making the ask."[4] In this model, making the ask begins with developing a statement that includes:

- why the organization or project deserves support, including how the organization or project aligns with the values of the donor;
- how funding the project will benefit both the donor and recipients; and
- how the project will solve a problem.[5]

Although "the ask" for a residency proposal is different from a fund raising proposal, many of the elements are the same. A request for residency support will:

- highlight the mission of the library and institution, emphasizing how a residency program aligns with the institution's values;
- show how creating the program will benefit the library, the larger campus or library system, and the recipients; and
- show how a residency program would solve a problem in the profession or the institution.

First, find the library's mission statement, as well as the mission statement of your university or larger organization. For example, the University of Utah's mission statement is

> to [foster] student success by preparing students from diverse backgrounds for lives of impact as leaders and citizens. We generate and share new knowledge, discoveries, and innovations, and we engage local and global communities to promote education, health, and quality of life. These contributions, in addition to responsible stewardship of our intellectual, physical, and financial resources, ensure the long-term success and viability of the institution.[6]

This mission motivates the four strategic goals: "Develop and transfer new knowledge, promote student success to transform lives, engage communities to improve health and quality of life, ensure long-term viability of the U."[7] The library, in turn, focuses on meeting these goals because it "inspires the creation, discovery, and use of knowledge for Utah and the world."[8] In your proposal, describe how implementing a residency program would help the institution meet each of these goals. Table 3.2 shows a similar process for the J. Willard Marriott Library at the University of Utah.

After participating in this process, you have the available material ready to format a proposal. Although there are many strategies for how to write a persuasive proposal, the NOSE format is easy to use and remember. The acronym NOSE stands for four parts to include in the proposal:

- state the *needs* of the organization,
- highlight the *outcomes* of solving the problem,
- offer a *solution*, and
- provide *evidence*.[9]

Another possible step that you may find helpful in the process of building a residency program is conducting an environmental scan of existing programs, including talking

Table 3.2. Example of How to Align Residency Program Goals with a University Mission Statement

MISSION STATEMENT	GOALS	GOALS
Fosters student success	Residencies help recent library students learn career skills to support their success	Residents contribute to teaching, outreach, and other projects that directly touch students' lives
Preparing students from diverse backgrounds	Residencies can encourage people from underrepresented groups to stay in librarianship	Resident can/will provide outreach to students from underrepresented groups on campus
For lives of impact as leaders and citizens	Residencies teach new librarians important leadership skills	Residents play an active role in educating future leaders to use information responsibly
Generate and share new knowledge, discoveries, and innovations	Residents give libraries an opportunity to learn about new developments in librarianship in order to better support students	Residents participate in the mission of helping students, faculty, and staff build and share new knowledge

with coordinators or residents of existing programs. See table 3.3 for a sample interview worksheet to use in an environmental scan interview with a residency organizer at another institution. This allows you to find out about what kinds of programs are out there, how they are run, and what has worked or not worked for them. Whether or not you incorporate what you find into your proposal, this can initiate you and your team into a community of practice for residency organizers. It may also help to have knowledge of other programs on hand as you deliver your proposal to administrative stakeholders.

For an example of how this proposal might look, see below:

SAMPLE PROPOSAL TO SUPPORT A DIVERSITY RESIDENCY PROGRAM

Background

The University of Utah's larger mission is to "foster student success by preparing students from diverse backgrounds for lives of impact as leaders and citizens ... generate and share new knowledge, discoveries, and innovations, and ... engage local and global communities to promote education, health, and quality of life."[10] Although the J. Willard Marriott Library has supported these goals through its mission to "inspire the creation, discovery, and use of knowledge for Utah and the world,"[11] we face new opportunities and challenges as we seek to support our students, faculty, and staff. Like others across the country, our university is growing more diverse, bringing in students with a variety of backgrounds, passions, and needs.[12]

Need

Despite the growth of diversity on our campuses, our profession is not growing apace; in 2012, the American Library Association published data showing that approximately 88 percent of librarians are white. Librarian demographics do not match up with the communities we serve.[13] In order to remedy this problem, we need to recruit and retain dedicated and energetic librarians ready to support students, faculty, and staff in meeting their intellectual goals and furthering the mission of the university. Such new professionals enable the library and university to better support students', faculty members', and staff members' learning and growth.

Proposal

A great strategy for meeting this need for qualified young professionals would be a residency program. As defined by ALISE, a library residency is "a post-degree work experience designed as an entry-level program for professionals who have recently received a graduate degree."[14] Residencies offer a number of benefits for both the residents and the institution. Residents learn real-world social, technical, and leadership skills, acquiring the professional experiences needed for many library positions. Such programs also support the retention of diverse librarians in the profession. Institutions who hire residents also benefit; these new professionals can reach out to students from a variety of backgrounds across campus, fostering student success by participating in teaching, outreach, and other projects that directly touch students' lives. Residents also offer libraries an opportunity to support multiple projects by bringing multiple residents in over time instead of hiring a single full-time person.

Next Steps

The library should explore this opportunity by appointing an ad hoc task force to determine what resources would be necessary to make the project a success, including funding and departmental support. Next, the Diversity and Inclusion Committee should collaborate with the Budget Committee to determine the exact amount of salary savings the library can expect in the next two years as well as the unallocated funds in the budget in order to confirm that we can successfully fund such a program.

Conclusions

Creating a library residency program at the J. Willard Marriott Library will allow us to better reach our goal of fostering the success of students, faculty, and staff by hiring excellent new librarians to complete short-term projects. In addition, we will have the opportunity to change even more new librarians' lives by allowing them to learn new skills, become socialized to the profession, and gain valuable professional experience.

Table 3.3. Sample Environmental Scan Interview Form

HOSTING INSTITUTION	LENGTH OF PROGRAM	LIBRARY TYPE	COHORT SIZE	ROTATIONS (Y/N)

Informational Interview Questions

How is recruitment performed for your residency program? If you are a resident, how did you find out about the program?

When and how is program assessment performed? How is/are the resident(s) involved in program assessment and evaluation?

What has worked well in your program? Are there aspects of the program that you have changed or would like to change?

How are the resident's professional goals met through the program?

How many people in your organization contribute to the program? How is communication among all parties ensured?

Share the Proposal

Once the proposal is ready to share, the next step is to schedule a conversation with the appropriate administrator or group to discuss the idea. Conversations of this type should include:

- a discussion of the goals of the institution and how the residency can support them,
- a short explanation of how the institution could implement the residency,
- a request for support, and
- a question-and-answer session.

Some of the phrases below might be useful for starting such a conversation:

1. Associate Dean X, I have really enjoyed being a part of the library's continued growth and success in the years I have been here. In particular, we have done a great job onboarding and integrating new employees into the library profession, which has enabled us to support students even better. One way we could continue to improve our support of students and enhance the library profession would be to consider a residency program.
2. Director X, I know both of us are very interested in how we can continue growing the library profession. Thanks to our excellent professional development work, we have done a great job promoting librarianship. Another strategy to increase our engagement in the profession would be to develop a residency.

At this point, provide a brief recapitulation of the proposal, emphasizing the benefits of the residency for the library and institution. Be as prepared as possible to answer questions the administrator asks. To prepare, review the list of potential concerns the stakeholder may have from above and consider how to best respond to those concerns. Some common questions from a dean or associate dean might be:

- Are any of our peer institutions doing similar programs?
- Why should we support a program like this when we are already low on funds for new hires?
- Would such a program add substantially to our work load?

Once the question-and-answer period concludes, thank the administrator for his or her time and ask about the appropriate follow-up steps. The administrator may want you to share the proposal with other stakeholder groups or to share it themselves. They may also have suggestions of other partners or groups to include in such discussions. They may also be able to suggest how you should plan to move forward, such as through creating an ad hoc committee to begin developing a plan or through some other mechanism. You may also want to speak with your administrator about who will take responsibility for the project. Will it be you, if you made the request, or another? Will you proceed as a team or individually?

What to Do if the Person Says No

It is possible that, despite your best efforts, the response to the proposal will be no. In this case, you should follow up to get a little bit more information about why the person is saying no. In some cases, it may be because of an easily solved concern. In other cases, the "no" might mean "not right now." If the administrator indicates that they would prefer to wait until later, make a plan to follow up and reschedule the conversation for later. Although such responses can be discouraging, they don't necessarily spell the end of a residency. An important note is that you should remember to follow up in the future when you said you will. Use the time between now and then to gather more information about other residencies at peer institutions or to respond to the concerns that your administrator raised. If the administrator has not refused the proposal but seems lackluster about it, ask for suggestions about who else you should contact in the library. There may be another department in your library that would have an interest in sponsoring such a program, even if your department or division cannot.

⑥ Find Grant Support

Another way to financially support a residency program is to apply for grant funding. In 2011, the University of Southern California received funding through the Institute of Museum and Library Services (IMLS) Laura Bush 21st-Century Librarian program to work with the Autry Museum Library and Archives and California State University, Northridge (CSUN) to host early-career residents. Each institution hosted one resident per year for two years, and the residents were responsible for working with various archives that were members of the L.A. as Subject research alliance.[15] In 2018, the IMLS provided funding for a second iteration of this program.[16] Although grant funding has been reduced in the current economy, searching for grant opportunities to support a residency program, even as a pilot, would still be valuable.

By telling the story of how a residency can fill a need in the library, the institution, and the profession and the resources necessary to make the project a reality, grants offer donors an opportunity to make a positive contribution to a project that aligns with their interests. One of the first steps, then, is to identify granting agencies with similar goals and interests. The Institute of Museum and Library Services (IMLS) offers many federal grants to library and museums and also allocates funds for states to offer Library Services and Technology Act (LSTA) grants.[17] Institutes or foundations interested in diversity, equity, and inclusion might also provide grant money. There are many online tools for locating grants. Your library or institution may also have professional grant writers who would be able to help you locate appropriate opportunities. For more information on this process, review Bess G. de Farber's book *Collaborative Grant-Seeking: A Practical Guide for Librarians*.

The next step at this point is to develop the grant application. Read the sponsor guidelines carefully and follow them to the letter. Even similar institutions may have very different guidelines. A good strategy to learn more about the funding institution is to review the applications that have been funded, when possible. De Farber recommends creating a checklist of all of the different portions of the grant application in the order the institution requests them.[18]

⑥ Communicate Program Goals

Another important step in building support for a residency is to develop a communication plan to share information about the residency to the stakeholders identified earlier in the process. In the sample timeline for developing a program below (table 3.4), organizers should ideally be ready to communicate about the residency program proposal to potential supervisors, funders, and mentors by at least three months before recruitment begins. Having a communication plan ready can take care of some of the logistical questions behind the acts of garnering internal support for the program. For example, will one person share the committee's work in a one-on-one meeting with an associate dean, dean, or director? Will you report out regularly to other library staff? How will you share your information? By building transparency into the project early, you may be able to avoid any frustration or dismay from people feeling like they did not get to participate in the process. Regular updates provide opportunities to solicit volunteers for specific roles, including people who would be willing to supervise a specific project for the resident, teach a new skill, or serve on a search committee. Others might be willing to serve as research mentors or as informal mentors to help the resident get used to the surrounding area. Asking for feedback often can also give you a chance to learn more about any concerns you need to address before the resident arrives to make the program a success.

Table 3.4. Sample Timeline for Pilot Residency Program Development

STAGE	TIME	STEPS
Research and environmental scan	1–3 months	Perform background research on residency programs
		Conduct environmental scan of existing residency programs
Develop program proposal and secure or plan support	3–12 months	Identify needed players and stakeholders within the organization and funders if needed
		Develop proposals for organizational stakeholders and funders
		Deliver proposals
Recruitment	1–3 months	Develop job ad
		Identify recruitment outlets and activities
		Post online job ads; conduct other recruitment activities
		Announce residency position and program to organization
Search and hire	1–4 months	Convene search committee
		Review applications
		First-round (phone) interviews
		Second-round (in-person) interviews
		Selection and offer
Onboarding prep	2–6 weeks	Notify direct players (Rotation 1 direct players at minimum)
		Communicate timeline and expectations to direct players
		Announce residency hire to organization
		Develop rotation/project timelines with area supervisors (Rotation 1 timeline at minimum)
		Pre-arrival communication with resident
		Undergo and/or refresh supervisory training and diversity training
Rotation 1	4 months	Organizational orientation
		Department orientation
		Ensure resident is assigned operational work and special projects in rotational work area as expected
		30-day and 3-month check-ins with resident
		Complete rotation/project timelines for Rotation 2

(continued)

Table 3.4. *Continued*

STAGE	TIME	STEPS
Rotation 2	4 months	Program assessment and evaluation based on Rotation 1
		Department orientation
		Ensure resident is assigned operational work and special projects in rotational work area as expected
		6-month check-in with resident
		Complete rotation/project timelines for Rotation 3
Rotation 3	4 months	Program assessment and evaluation based on Rotation 2
		Department orientation
		Ensure resident is assigned operational work and special projects in rotational work area as expected
		Complete timeline and scoping for yearlong residency project
Residency project	12 months	12-month check-in; program assessment and evaluation based on Rotation 3
		Ensure project resources
		Ensure targeted mentorship for job search process
		Summative program assessment and evaluation
		Begin planning and recruitment for next resident/cohort

Key Points

Developing support from key stakeholders and outside partners is an essential part of developing a residency program. When planning a residency program, consider these key points:

- Identify stakeholders, their needs and wants, and the resources they can provide to the program early in the process.
- Develop a proposal describing the need for a residency program, the benefits for the stakeholders involved, and the resources and tools necessary to implement it.
- Have a conversation with administration to share your proposals and to answer any questions and concerns, making sure to follow up as needed.
- Apply for grants and develop outside partnerships to support the financial goals of the residency.
- Make a plan to communicate with stakeholders throughout the program development.

Notes

1. R. Edward Freeman, *Strategic Management: A Stakeholder Approach* (Cambridge: Cambridge University Press, 2010), vi.
2. Pernille Eskerod and Martina Huemann, *Rethink! Project Stakeholder Management* (Newtown Square, Pa.: Project Management Institute, 2016).

3. Ibid.

4. Laura Fredricks, *The Ask: How to Ask for Support for Your Nonprofit Cause, Creative Project, or Business Venture* (Newark, N.J.: John Wiley & Sons, 2009), xix.

5. Ibid., 25.

6. University of Utah and President Ruth Watkins, "University Strategy," accessed November 12, 2018, president.utah.edu/universitystrategy/.

7. Ibid.

8. J. Willard Marriott Library, University of Utah, "Our Mission, Vision and Values," accessed November 12, 2018, lib.utah.edu/info/mission.php.

9. Tom Sant, *Persuasive Business Proposals: Writing to Win More Customers, Clients, and Contracts* (New York: Amacom, 2012), 31.

10. University of Utah and Watkins, "University Strategy."

11. J. Willard Marriott Library, University of Utah, "Our Mission, Vision and Values."

12. Angela Boyd, Yolanda Blue, and Suzanne Im, "Evaluation of Academic Library Residency Programs in the United States for Librarians of Color," *College & Research Libraries* 78, no. 4 (2017): 472–511, doi:10.5860/crl.78.4.472.

13. "Diversity Counts," *About ALA*, March 29, 2007, www.ala.org/aboutala/offices/diversity/diversitycounts/divcounts.

14. Julie Brewer, ed., *Internship, Residency, and Fellowship Programs in ARL Libraries* (Washington, D.C.: Association of Research Libraries, Office of Management Services, 1992), 67.

15. University of Southern California, "LA as Subject Residency Program 2014–2017," *LA as Subject*, October 17, 2018, laassubject.org/residency-program/la-subject-residency-program-2014-2017.

16. Bill Dotson, "IMLS Awards Laura Bush 21st Century Librarian Grant to Support L.A. as Subject Digital Residency and Training Program," *USC Libraries*, August 29, 2018, libraries.usc.edu/article/imls-awards-laura-bush-21st-century-librarian-grant-support-la-as-subject-digital-residency.

17. Bess G. De Farber, *Collaborative Grant-Seeking: A Practical Guide for Librarians* (Lanham, Md.: Rowman & Littlefield, 2016), 62–63.

18. De Farber, *Collaborative Grant-Seeking*.

◎ References

Boyd, Angela, Yolanda Blue, and Suzanne Im. "Evaluation of Academic Library Residency Programs in the United States for Librarians of Color." *College & Research Libraries* 78, no. 4 (2017): 472–511. doi:10.5860/crl.78.4.472.

Brewer, Julie, ed. *Internship, Residency, and Fellowship Programs in ARL Libraries*. Washington, D.C.: Association of Research Libraries, Office of Management Services, 1992.

De Farber, Bess G. *Collaborative Grant-Seeking: A Practical Guide for Librarians*. Lanham, Md.: Rowman & Littlefield, 2016.

"Diversity Counts." *About ALA*, March 29, 2007. /www.ala.org/aboutala/offices/diversity/diversity counts/divcounts.

Dotson, Bill. "IMLS Awards Laura Bush 21st Century Librarian Grant to Support L.A. as Subject Digital Residency and Training Program." *USC Libraries*, August 29, 2018. libraries.usc.edu/article/imls-awards-laura-bush-21st-century-librarian-grant-support-la-as-subject-digital-residency.

Eskerod, Pernille, and Martina Huemann. *Rethink! Project Stakeholder Management*. Newtown Square, Pa.: Project Management Institute, 2016.

Fredricks, Laura. *The Ask: How to Ask for Support for Your Nonprofit Cause, Creative Project, or Business Venture*. Newark, N.J.: John Wiley & Sons, 2009.

Freeman, R. Edward. *Strategic Management: A Stakeholder Approach.* Cambridge: Cambridge University Press, 2010.

J. Willard Marriott Library, University of Utah. "Our Mission, Vision and Values." Accessed November 12, 2018. lib.utah.edu/info/mission.php.

Sant, Tom. *Persuasive Business Proposals: Writing to Win More Customers, Clients, and Contracts.* New York: Amacom, 2012.

University of Southern California. "LA as Subject Residency Program 2014–2017." *LA as Subject,* October 17, 2018. laassubject.org/residency-program/la-subject-residency-program-2014-2017.

University of Utah and President Ruth Watkins. "University Strategy." Accessed November 12, 2018. president.utah.edu/universitystrategy/.

CHAPTER 4

Developing a Plan for the Residency

IN THIS CHAPTER

▷ Using Backward Design in Residency Planning

▷ Defining a Vision of Success for the Residency

▷ Creating Learning Objectives for the Residency

▷ Designing Learning Activities

▷ Gathering Resources

▷ Putting the Process into Action

DESIGNING AN EFFECTIVE RESIDENCY represents a key challenge for residency planners and managers. Although residents are professionally credentialed and prepared to take on the responsibilities of librarianship, many are new professionals who come to residencies looking for structured experiences to explore multiple aspects of librarianship. To meet this expectation, residency planners must engage in careful preparation, monitoring, and adjustment in order to help residents build and strengthen core competencies that will help them meet their future career goals while also meeting the needs of the host institution.

Using Backward Design in Residency Planning

Backward design offers a useful framework for the planning process. Backward design encourages curriculum designers to develop learning objectives first, make a plan for how to best assess these objectives, and then design learning activities that will enable students to complete the assessments. Backward design advocates beginning with the intended outcomes and then developing a strategy to meet them.[1] Although the backward design process was originally designed for a classroom experience and not for planning professional development, many of the concepts in it are valuable in developing a plan for the residency. Although the plan for the residency will likely shift over time to accommodate changes, having a plan from the beginning will help the institution and the resident see the comprehensive scope and arc of the residency.

Many are tempted to begin developing a residency plan by identifying activities or projects for residents and then considering how to fit these projects together into a cohesive development experience. Focusing on projects or activities first, however, may mean that the residency doesn't have the strategic focus necessary to give the resident a cohesive learning experience. Instead, developing a comprehensive plan for the residency involves beginning with a strong sense of the goals of the residency. Residency planners should begin the development process by:

- identifying a vision of success;
- developing learning goals or core competencies for residents, supervisors, and other stakeholders based on the vision of success, focusing on the knowledge, skills, and abilities needed to meet these core competencies;
- planning learning or professional development activities to help meet these learning goals or core competencies;
- gathering together the necessary tools and resources to implement learning activities; and
- developing assessment and feedback mechanisms to assess how these goals have been met.

⑥ Defining a Vision of Success for the Residency

The first step in the backward design process is defining a high-level vision of what success would look like for the institution, the resident, and the stakeholders. Success for the institution will likely be defined by meeting the mission and strategic goals of the institution as described in chapter 3. For instance, one of the University of Utah's strategic goals is to foster student success, and table 3.2 demonstrates that the resident can help meet this goal by contributing to outreach and teaching. Therefore, a vision of success would include a resident actively involved in outreach and teaching. At the same time, it is important to consider elements of success for the institution or library that may fall outside of the goals. For example, some of these goals might be based on the benefits elaborated in chapter 2, such as having a strong rapport with MLIS graduate programs and new professional communities or supporting the profession as a whole. Here are some potential goals for your institution that you might consider. Note that many of these goals could be an outcome of other goals listed in the process.

- Resident will be able to encourage future residents to apply for the residency position.
- Resident will be able to talk about the benefits of the program and the institution.
- Resident will continue in the profession.
- Resident will get the kind of job they want as a result of participating in the residency.

Table 4.1. Example of Stakeholders and Their Goals for the Residency

STAKEHOLDER	POTENTIAL GOALS FOR THE RESIDENCY
Friends of the Library	Creating positive publicity for the library and institution because the resident promotes the program
Student Services	Developing a partnership for further outreach to students
Library Schools	Supporting opportunities for new librarians to develop skills Encouraging retention of new librarians in the profession
State Libraries and Professional Organizations	Creating positive publicity for the state in order to encourage librarians to apply for jobs there Developing the profession by training new librarians

Stakeholders both in and outside of the organization might have additional goals that are different than those of the institution. For instance, friends of the library or the library advisory board might have positive publicity for the library as a goal. Other stakeholders on campus, like Student Services, might have an additional outreach partner as a goal. Only you will know for sure which of these goals are meaningful to the stakeholders that you identified in chapter 3. One potential way to get further feedback at this juncture is to ask them directly what their goals for the residency are, especially during the planning process.

The next step is defining the institution's vision of a successful residency cycle, encompassing the duration of one resident's time at the institution. For many institutions, this high-level vision of success likely includes contributing actively to the mission of the university, learning more about the function and roles of the different departments in the library as well as the function of the departments on campus, participating in professional development activities that develop core competencies in the resident's area of interest, learning professional skills, and finding a job in librarianship.

⑥ Creating Learning Objectives for the Residency

Once you have developed this vision of success, the next step is to break it down into specific objectives or competencies for the resident. Core competencies are defined as "the knowledge, skills, attitudes and personal attributes that enable people to succeed in a given environment."[2] For example, the ALA's *Guidelines for Behavioral Performance of Reference and Information Service Providers* functions as a list of core competencies for library employees that provide reference and information services, outlining the knowledge, skills, and abilities necessary to succeed in this role.[3] These competencies also function as learning objectives in backward design, enabling the resident and stakeholders to understand the desired outcomes for the residency. In many cases, residents will likely have their own core competencies that they want to gain, which can be incorporated in this process.

Defining learning outcomes or competencies begins by considering questions like: What will the resident know and be able to do as a result of participating in the residency? If the resident participates in a project, what will the resident be able to do as a result of participating in the project? Although this question initially seems simple, designing effective learning objectives takes time and careful consideration. Some may be broad in scope, such as knowing and being able to describe how the departments of the library work together to best support patrons. Many of your learning goals may be clustered together around the activities of a specific department. Others may be based on specific knowledge, skills, and abilities, such as being able to complete a cataloging process, that span multiple departments. You should also think about competencies that are necessary but not specific to librarianship, such as public speaking. As much as possible, the resident should be involved in developing learning goals and outcomes as well.

It is tempting to frame learning objectives very generally, such as "understand how the library works." However, the problem with such objectives is that it will be hard to assess whether the resident has actually met the goal because it is hard to measure how well someone understands something. Instead, be precise and choose action verbs that are measurable or result in a deliverable, such as "develop" or "prepare." One helpful resource in this process is Bloom's Taxonomy, which describes how to use measurable action verbs when creating learning objectives.[4]

Table 4.2. Action Verbs in Bloom's Taxonomy

LEARNING OBJECTIVE	DEFINITION	SAMPLE ACTION VERBS	
Knowledge	Familiarity with previously learned information	arrange, define, describe, duplicate, identify, label, list, match, memorize, name, order, outline, recognize, relate, recall, repeat, reproduce, select, state	
Comprehension	Understanding the meaning of information	classify, convert, defend, discuss, distinguish, estimate, explain, express, extend, generalize, give example(s), identify, indicate, infer, locate, paraphrase, predict, recognize, rewrite, report, restate, review, select, summarize, translate	
Application	Applying knowledge to theoretical and practical situations	apply, change, choose, compute, demonstrate, discover, dramatize, employ, illustrate, interpret, manipulate, modify, operate, practice, predict, prepare, produce, relate, schedule, show, sketch, solve, use, write	
Analysis	Detailed examination of the elements or structure of something, typically as a basis for discussion or interpretation	analyze, appraise, break down, calculate, categorize, classify, compare, contrast, criticize, derive, diagram, differentiate, discriminate, distinguish, examine, experiment, identify, illustrate, infer, interpret, model, outline, point out, question, relate, select, separate, subdivide, test	
Synthesis	Combining ideas into a new whole	arrange, assemble, categorize, collect, combine, comply, compose, construct, create, design, develop, devise, explain, formulate, generate, plan, prepare, propose, rearrange, reconstruct, relate, reorganize, revise, rewrite, set up, summarize, synthesize, tell, write	
Evaluation	Making judgments based on internal evidence or external criteria	appraise, argue, assess, attach, choose, compare, conclude, contrast, defend, describe, discriminate, estimate, evaluate, explain, interpret, judge, justify, predict, rate, relate, select, summarize, support, value	

Using Bloom's Taxonomy Verb Chart, you can clarify what the resident will be able to do as a result of the learning activity. For example, a resident working on a project about applying metadata might have a learning goal of being able to *transform* metadata. However, this goal is still vague. In order to clarify and further refine learning goals, one should measure the goal against SMART criteria. Is the learning objective or goal:

- Specific,
- Measurable,
- Achievable,
- Relevant, and
- Timebound?[5]

With regard to the goal above of transforming metadata, making the goal specific, measurable, achievable, relevant, and timely enables the resident and residency planners to have more clarity about the goal. A concrete version of this goal might be: "By the end of the resident's first six months, they will be able to *transform* archival metadata in EADXML to a format compatible with the digital library *with* XSLT code and *in order to enhance* the quality of metadata currently in the system."

Once the residency objectives have been defined, the next step is to think through how you will determine that the objectives have been met. Will the resident be able to perform a specific task or set of tasks? Will the resident be able to describe a process or idea? Ideally, the residents should demonstrate that they meet the objectives through participating in a project or activity that allows them to create a deliverable. The goal of most residencies is to enable residents to find full-time employment in librarianship, and giving them projects with deliverables enables them to show potential employers their skills. In addition, projects with deliverables allow the resident to experience all of the challenges associated with managing a project, giving them real-world skills. Multiple assessments may be necessary for the resident to demonstrate that they have met the objectives. We will discuss the process of developing assessments in more detail in chapter 9.

Designing Learning Activities

After developing the assessments, the next step is to develop learning activities. Learning activities include all of those activities where the resident will learn and practice skills. For example, learning activities might include completing training programs, shadowing another person or group, or completing parts of a project under the supervision of another person. For example, the contributor at the end of this chapter, a former resident, participated in several projects that provided strong learning activities related to archives. For a learning objective that asks the resident to describe the function of Special Collections and how it works with other departments in the library, learning activities might include a tour of Special Collections, participating in departmental meetings to learn more about how the department works, and reviewing the organizational chart and departmental workflows with a mentor. In many cases, learning activities will be training or a form of supervised practice. It is also important to remember that learning is ongoing and may require multiple learning or professional development activities as the resident progresses.

◉ Gathering Resources

Once the learning activities have been determined, the next step is to gather the appropriate resources to enact the learning opportunity. Resources needed may include paid or free training programs, specialized software and hardware, or books or articles. People are also another important resource to consider; in many cases, meeting with experts for training or discussion is an important learning activity for residents. It is also important to talk to the resident about whether they have access to other resources that might help them learn new skills.

Table 4.3. Example Backward Design Planning Table

LEARNING OBJECTIVE	PROJECT/ DELIVERABLE	LEARNING ACTIVITY	TRAINING/ PLANNING NEEDED
Resident will be able to describe the functions of Special Collections, its internal structure division and between other divisions, particularly the digital library.	Resident will explain the functions of Special Collections to the Head of Special Collections.	Tour of Special Collections Meeting with representative of each department Discussion with Head of Special Collections	Schedule a tour of Special Collections. Schedule meetings with heads of each functional area for an informational interview.
Resident will be able to assign basic copyright statements to photographs and digital collections in Special Collections.	Resident will create a written flow chart to describe what kind of rights statement to apply depending on the copyright status of a photograph or item in a digital collection.	Copyright review with Special Collections librarian	Schedule meetings with Special Collections librarian.
Resident will be able to create basic metadata for individual items and complete collections in Special Collections.	Resident will create an EAD access tool for a photograph collection and crosswalk that metadata to a format suitable for the digital library.	Training with archivist who currently creates EAD finding aids for photographs	Contact archivist who will do training and schedule training sessions, helping to facilitate and provide whatever materials are needed.

◉ Putting the Process into Action

The backward design process is useful at many levels throughout the residency planning process. For example, you may decide to develop a high-level set of learning objectives and activities for the program as a whole, which should then guide the development of projects for the resident. If one of the major outcomes for the residency is "the resident has work experience in each of the major departments in the library in order to explore multiple aspects of librarianship," this would dictate learning activities in each of the major departments. From this point, more refined backward planning for each project in each department can provide greater detail on the steps required to make the project a success.

The backward design process also makes it possible to develop an appropriate timeline for the resident's projects. For example, understanding how much training the resident needs enables residency planners to estimate how long the training will take. Then they can estimate how much time the resident will have for other learning activities, including completing the project. These estimates are important in making sure that the resident can complete the project effectively.

MENTORSHIP, THE COHORT EXPERIENCE, ROTATIONS, AND PROFESSIONAL DEVELOPMENT AS KEYS TO A SUCCESSFUL RESIDENCY EXPERIENCE, AN AUTOETHNOGRAPHY

by Joanna Chen Cham

My name is Joanna Chen Cham. I am a second-generation Taiwanese American librarian/archivist/digital humanist born and raised in Los Angeles. I am passionate about preserving history, creative storytelling, critical pedagogy, social justice, and diversity. And that is why, in the fall of 2015, I was thrilled and relieved to accept a full-time position at the University of Southern California (USC) as one of three Los Angeles as Subject (LAAS) Resident Archivists in the second cohort of the Los Angeles as Subject Residency Program funded by the Institute for Museum and Library Services (IMLS).

As an Angeleno who had worked in museums, archives, and libraries, I was excited to have the opportunity to utilize my professional background, newly obtained MLIS, and knowledge of the local community to play a role in preserving and documenting Los Angeles history as the USC Resident Archivist for L.A. as Subject, a research alliance of more than two hundred libraries, museums, archives, and private collectors with collections on the history and culture of Los Angeles. As an aspiring archivist at the time, I was also particularly grateful to be chosen for such a unique yearlong archives residency that would give me the opportunity to work on several different quarter-long projects at different types of institutions while having the support of a LAAS coordinator, Cindy Mediavilla; a host mentor/supervisor, which in my case was Claude Zachary at USC; my two fellow LAAS Resident Archivists at Autry Museum Library and Archives and California State University, Northridge (CSUN) Libraries, Stella Castillo and Amelia Parks; our Principal Investigator, Marje Schuetze-Coburn at USC; and a generous $2,000 professional development stipend.

The residency began with an orientation for all three of us Resident Archivists, along with our coordinator and mentors/supervisors, to discuss the structure of the program. At the heart of the program was the LAAS projects chosen to be our rotation sites. We each started with our host institution and then moved on each quarter throughout Southern California.

I began at USC, where I was able to initiate and propose a Taiwanese American Digital Archive initiative in collaboration with USC Special Collections and the East Asian Library in order to preserve the history of a large but often overlooked and otherwise subsumed community. Unlike the rotation sites that had set projects, my rotation project at USC was somewhat more flexible because it was at my host institution and because I had already previously worked at USC as an Association of Research Libraries and Society of American Archivists Mosaic Fellow during my MLIS and built relationships and trust with my colleagues there, which allowed me to propose and pursue the initiative as my rotation project. By the quarter's end, with the help of my father and the local Taiwanese American community, I had conducted a documentation strategy to research the status of Taiwanese American historical records; conducted outreach to local community members and leaders to assess collection development opportunities and to build support for beginning the Taiwanese American Digital Archive; facilitated donation and digitization discussions for a seed collection between *Pacific Times*, a national Taiwanese American newspaper, and USC, regarding never-before digitized 1987–2010 newspapers; organized a Taiwanese American Digital Archive Forum and Exhibit, which drew students, staff, faculty, and community support and attendance and was featured on NBC Asian America and *Pacific Times*; contributed to social media content for general outreach; participated in a digital scholarship working group with USC Libraries faculty and staff; and provided drop-in reference services to staff, students, and faculty from a diverse campus population. It was an exciting and ambitious way to start the residency and gave me the opportunity to start a project from scratch and build support by working with different campus groups as well as the local community.

My second rotation was at Occidental College Special Collections, a private liberal arts college, where I processed and created a finding aid for a local photographer's collection of more than one hundred thousand photographic negatives in ArchivesSpace; researched and assessed collection condition and rehoused collection with suggestions for future steps; collaborated with the Center for Digital Liberal Arts to conduct donor oral history interviews; curated a digital exhibition of selected representative photographs in Omeka to increase accessibility; and gave an on-campus presentation on "Creating Access to Local History and Community Collections," accompanied by a library exhibit, which was well attended by campus staff, LAAS members, and the local community and was featured in the Eagle Rock Valley Historical Society Newsletter. At Oxy, I enjoyed the opportunity to work in yet another environment, this time with a much smaller liberal arts college and Special Collections staff, and gained both more processing experience with ArchivesSpace as well as more experience incorporating digital humanities (in the form of oral histories and digital exhibits) as part of adding more context to a collection and public outreach.

My third rotation was at the Wende Museum, a museum dedicated to preserving Cold War history, where I primarily worked on an archival collection of Soviet Hippies materials to implement new archival processing workflow by mapping archival standards to MimsyXG database fields in order to best mirror ArchivesSpace in collaboration with the Collections Department; created documentation and training tools for future archival processing staff and interns; streamlined the archival description process by creating a Google Form to gather background information from donors at the start of the acquisition process; and researched and recommended preservation resources for collections care and disaster preparation. Working with collections in a museum setting again, where workflows and software and needs differ from the traditional academic setting, gave me the opportunity to experience collections outside of what I had become used to and gave me the experience I needed to be confident that I can quickly learn and adapt to new software and workflows, as well as create new workflows and programs with whatever staff time and tools I am given.

For full disclosure, I ended up finding a full-time permanent Lead for Emerging Literacies Librarian position at the University of California, Los Angeles

(UCLA) afterward and ended my residency one rotation early with the support of the LAAS, with much gratitude for the opportunities I had. During our yearlong LAAS Residency, we met once a month as a cohort with our residency coordinator, at each of our rotation sites per quarter. Each time, we would discuss logistics, highlights, and challenges with the projects at each of our rotation sites, and it became a valuable time of sharing ideas and encouragement as we sought to complete ambitious projects in the short amount of time we had. We also met with Cindy and our own mentors regularly throughout each rotation, in order to ensure we were getting the support we needed to complete each rotation successfully.

As a way to involve the larger LAAS community and general public, we were also each required to conduct at least one formal or informal program or workshop per rotation. We were also highly encouraged to attend and present at conferences and given a generous $2,000 professional development stipend for the year.

Looking back now, I absolutely, firmly believe that my LAAS Resident Archivist experience helped to jump-start my professional career. Entering a residency at the start of my post-MLIS career, especially one where I worked at multiple institutions and was part of a larger research alliance, gave me the opportunity to experience and adapt to different types of environments and workflows at each rotation site while packing in a number of intense projects that allowed me to grow my experience and build my skills in: working with donors and local communities, creating and documenting new workflows, processing and rehousing collections, learning and using different types of software, conducting outreach through programming and social media, providing reference services, and giving presentations to the campus, archives, and local communities.

As one of the roughly 4 percent of Asian American Pacific Islander librarians nationwide and of only 1 percent of Asian American archivists nationwide, the residency also gave me the opportunity to network widely at each rotation site and at LAAS meetings. To date, one of the things I love most about working in the information science profession is how generous and supportive people in the profession can be, and as someone who didn't know anyone in the profession before I entered the field, it was wonderful to start my post-MLIS career in a way that introduced me to many other individuals and institutions as part of my residency/job.

The mentorship, peer cohort, and the expectation as well as the financial support to engage in and pursue professional development were also critical to my success in finding full-time employment after my residency experience. As a student, I was blessed and am grateful to have found those same elements of support through being an ALA Spectrum Scholar and ARL Fellow. Participating in a residency that understood and valued mentorship and the cohort experience and both encouraged and financially supported professional development was huge—especially in a field where positions for early-career professionals can often be part-time, grant-funded, contracted, or otherwise have very limited or no professional development support. I loved presenting and sharing what I learned at the end of each rotation, and the experience of that, as well as the $2,000 stipend, propelled me forward to move from conference attendee to conference presenter.

With the support of my mentors, local presentation experience, and the security of knowing I had financial support for my endeavors, I both initiated and joined conference panel proposals throughout the year. By the end of my residency, I had four conference presentations under my belt in four national conferences: "Serving up the Subversive" at ALA Annual, "Working for Tomorrow: Student Activism, Education, and Diversity in the Archives" at SAA Annual, "ARL Diversity Fellows Around the Fireplace: Lived Experiences and Lessons Learned" at the National Diversity in Libraries Conference, and "Archiving Taiwanese American History: The Time is Now" at the Taiwanese American West Coast Conference. Through a combination of finding alternative modes of transportation, staying with friends, budgeting meals, saving, and utilizing all of my professional development stipend, I was able to attend all four conferences in Orlando, Atlanta, Los Angeles, and Foster City. It was an intense and busy summer of presenting and attending conferences, but it was magical to take the first step in giving back to the profession by sharing what I had learned and insights I had gained and to continue to connect and network with so many amazing and talented colleagues nationwide. Adding four national conference presentations to my CV was also critical in demonstrating to my future employer that I was eager to learn and could contribute to the field as an early-career professional.

I cannot stress this enough, but for me, it was all the aspects of the residency—the mentorship, peer cohort support, varied rotation environments and projects, and professional development encouragement and stipend—that allowed me to succeed in finding a full-time, permanent position after the residency and jumpstart my professional career. Without any of those key elements, the residency experience would have been vastly different, but together, the residency gave me the keys I needed to succeed.

If there is anything I have learned since entering this profession, it is that we are not alone and that we succeed by leaning on and helping each other. The LAAS Residency created a program and structure that embraced this sentiment by providing mentors I could learn from and confide in while tackling each new project; peers I could grow with and bounce ideas off of; varied rotation experiences and workflows that allowed me to gain critical hands-on experience in different environments and settings; and presentation expectations and a generous professional development stipend that built my confidence and gave me the financial support I needed to start giving back to the profession. For this, I am most grateful.

Key Points

- Backward design, which includes developing learning outcomes, designing assessments, defining learning activities, and determining needed resources, is a useful model for planning the residency and its associated projects.
- Defining clear and specific learning objectives, as well as appropriate learning activities and assessments, can help make sure that the resident's professional development is useful and appropriate.

⊚ Notes

1. Grant P. Wiggins, and Jay McTighe, *Understanding by Design*, expanded 2nd ed. (Alexandria, Va.: Association for Supervision and Curriculum Development, 2005).
2. Lorelei Rutledge et al., "Competency-Based Talent Management: Three Perspectives in an Academic Library," *Journal of Library Administration* 56, no. 3 (2016): 235–50.
3. Reference and User Services Association, "Guidelines for Behavioral Performance of Reference and Information Service Providers," *Reference & User Services Association (RUSA)*, September 29, 2008, www.ala.org/rusa/resources/guidelines/guidelinesbehavioral.
4. Benjamin Samuel Bloom, *Taxonomy of Educational Objectives: The Classification of Educational Goals*. New York: Longman, 1984.
5. George T. Doran, "There's a SMART Way to Write Management's Goals and Objectives," *Management Review* 70, no. 11 (1981): 35–36.

⊚ References

Bloom, Benjamin Samuel. *Taxonomy of Educational Objectives: The Classification of Educational Goals*. New York: Longman, 1984.

Doran, George T. "There's a SMART Way to Write Management's Goals and Objectives." *Management Review* 70, no. 11 (1981): 35–36.

Reference and User Services Association. "Guidelines for Behavioral Performance of Reference and Information Service Providers." *Reference & User Services Association (RUSA)*, September 29, 2008. www.ala.org/rusa/resources/guidelines/guidelinesbehavioral.

Rutledge, Lorelei, Sarah LeMire, Melanie Hawks, and Alfred Mowdood. "Competency-Based Talent Management: Three Perspectives in an Academic Library." *Journal of Library Administration* 56, no. 3 (2016): 235–50.

Wiggins, Grant P., and Jay McTighe. *Understanding by Design*. Expanded 2nd ed. Alexandria, Va.: Association for Supervision and Curriculum Development, 2005.

CHAPTER 5

Developing the Administrative Structure for a Residency

IN THIS CHAPTER

▷ Developing Appropriate Administrative Structure

▷ Assigning Residency Roles

▷ Defining the Resident's Role in the Organization

HAPTER 4 DISCUSSED THE NEED to develop effective learning outcomes in order to build a comprehensive residency program. Developing outcomes enables the resident and residency planners to develop a plan to meet them, gathering appropriate people and resources. However, at the same time these outcomes are being developed, it is important to consider what kind of administrative structure is required to manage the tools and resources needed for the residency effectively.

Developing Appropriate Administrative Structure

When considering the scope of the residency, an important consideration is where the resident will be placed in the organization. Making this decision involves considering a number of important questions, such as:

- Will a single person or a team be in charge of designing and administering the residency?
- Will the resident work in a single department or multiple departments?
- If the resident does rotations, will they still have a single supervisor, or will they switch supervisors?

- Who will supervise the resident? Will supervision duties be assigned to the current head of a department, or will another library employee serve as the supervisor?
- What other kinds of support people will the resident need to be successful?

One useful way to begin addressing these questions is to consider the project roles that will need to be filled when designing a residency.

Assigning Residency Roles

Like all new employees, residents need appropriate socialization to the work environment. In order to complete the socialization process effectively, residents need a strong support network throughout the organization. An effective administrative structure enables the development of this strong support network. Four major roles in this support network are:

- Residency Coordinator: An individual responsible for coordinating the residency, sharing information about the goals of the residency, encouraging Project/Resource Coordinators to develop projects, and serving in an assessment role as needed for the program, supervisor, project/resource coordinators, and resident.
- Supervisor(s): Individual(s) responsible for managing the direct work of the resident and providing daily support. The supervisor usually also takes on an assessment role in determining whether the resident meets learning goals or core competencies.
- Project/Resource Coordinators: Individual(s) in each department or area where the resident will work who are responsible for defining a project (in consultation with the resident), providing the resident with appropriate training, and providing feedback and assessment on the resident's learning.
- Mentors: Individuals both in and outside of the library who provide the resident with support in navigating the institutional and departmental cultures. Unlike the other roles, the mentor is usually not responsible for any kind of formal assessment of the resident and instead provides support to the resident and feedback about the program.

Throughout this chapter, we discuss different elements of each of the roles, as well as strategies for filling them.

Residency Coordinator

Assigning a residency coordinator to serve as the point person throughout the planning and development of the program ensures that the many tasks necessary to make the program successful are complete. The coordinator or manager can play several roles. For example, the University of Utah J. Willard Marriott Library's residency coordinator has responsibilities such as:

- Preparing and submitting institutional paperwork for the resident
  - Assisting the Residency Task Force with development of the resident job posting
  - Posting the position with appropriate approvals while working with the appropriate Human Resources professional

- Creating a website and other promotional materials to advertise the residency
- Coordinating the onboarding of the resident

- Scheduling all components of the residency program for the first year by working with "area advisors" in each major department to:

  - Develop learning outcomes and deliverables for projects
  - Develop a timeline and work calendar for each library area and project.

- Meeting with the area advisors and the resident on a regular basis
- Arranging for tours, workshops, or introductions to other library professionals based on the resident's interests
- Using information gathered from assessments to prepare a report describing the successes and areas for program improvement
- Staying abreast of current trends in the library profession at the state and national level in order to support the resident in developing cutting-edge skills

Although most of these tasks are a group effort between supervisors, department heads, and project/resource coordinators, a single high-level coordinator can organize these tasks and make sure they are completed in a timely manner.

Supervisor

In addition to having someone act in the role of residency coordinator, the program coordinator and anyone else involved in residency planning must also determine how the resident's day-to-day work will be supervised. If the resident will be based in a single department, then a supervisor in that department will likely be the best fit. This relationship will likely remain stable throughout the residency. On the other hand, the resident may be rotating between departments. In this case, it may make sense to have the resident in a single home department with the same stable reporting structure, or it may make sense to have the resident rotate supervisors as they move through departments.

Like any supervisor, the residency supervisor will have the same major roles to play, such as

- supporting the development of knowledge, skills, and abilities to meet required and preferred job qualifications;
- monitoring the day-to-day work of the resident, providing regular feedback; and
- working with the resident to plan professional development opportunities.

There are multiple strategies to finding the appropriate supervisor. Hiring someone for the position who has this supervision role as part of ongoing responsibilities ensures the institution has someone prepared to manage the resident. Another option may be to have the resident report directly to the supervisor in their home department. Opening the opportunity to other current members of the organization who may want to explore supervision also creates a professional development opportunity for another person.

Project Coordinator

Another important person to consider in designing a plan for supervision is a project coordinator. A project coordinator can take on the important role of working with the resident, the residency coordinator, and/or the resident's supervisor to help with developing learning goals for projects in specific specialized areas. The project coordinator can help provide specialized training to residents. For a resident interested in metadata, a skilled metadata librarian who can train them and supervise a metadata project would be extremely helpful, even if the regular supervisor is a librarian in another department or area. Even if the resident changes supervisors each time they change rotations, having area advisors or project coordinators allows the resident to have learning experiences with specialists in different departments or areas of the library without requiring that the specialists take on the full role of the supervisor.

At the University of Utah J. Willard Marriott Library, the project coordinator role is filled by area advisors. The role of the area advisor is to work with the residency program coordinator to plan and implement a resident's experience during their time in the advisor's area of expertise. Advisors are responsible for:

- structuring the resident's project with appropriate learning goals to outcomes developed mutually between the area advisor, supervisor, resident, and/or coordinator;
- answering questions and providing domain-specific knowledge to the resident as needed;
- helping the resident connect with the rest of the department;
- developing a timeline and work calendar for the resident;
- adhering to their portion of the resident's schedule and communicating with the program coordinator regarding any schedule or content changes;
- providing an orientation to their area;
- creating appropriate training opportunities in their department;
- overseeing the resident's work and having weekly meetings with the resident to discuss progress;
- facilitating at least one informal session for the resident to give an informal presentation on what they have learned, recent literature, and current projects relating to their work in the department;
- preparing a performance evaluation of the resident's work and submitting it to the program coordinator;
- bringing any issues or problems related to the residency to the attention of the program coordinator; and
- participating in an interview with the program coordinator to evaluate the residency program and to recommend any changes

Mentor

Mentors will also play an important role throughout the resident's time in the program. Although residents will likely find informal mentors in the organization, consider assigning a formal mentor, particularly one outside the resident's assigned department(s). The mentor can play an important role in helping the resident understand the structure and culture of the library and also serves as a resource in addition to the resident's supervisor.

The role of the mentor is to work with the resident to help the resident translate their two-year experience to an outside audience. At the University of Utah's J. Willard Marriott Library, the mentor has multiple roles and is responsible for:

- ongoing communication, at least once a month, with the resident to share insights, review assignments, provide constructive feedback and evaluation, and provide opportunities for problem solving and troubleshooting;
- arranging for tours, workshops, and introductions on campus—these should be especially focused on helping the resident get connected on campus, especially to other diversity programs on campus and meeting other new hires;
- assisting the resident with translating their experience to an outside focus, such as a presentation, poster, or publication;
- assisting the resident with selection of a capstone project(s) for the second year;
- assisting with wording for the resident's curriculum vitae regarding the residency program;
- providing editing assistance for the resident's curriculum vitae and cover letters, particularly with a description of the residency program;
- assisting the resident in identifying career goals and aspirations and connecting them to the appropriate professional organizations;
- assisting the resident with the job search in the second half of the second year;
- guiding the resident through the recruitment and interviewing process;
- bringing any issues or problems to the attention of the residency program coordinator; and
- participating in an interview with the program coordinator to evaluate the residency program and to recommend any changes.

These are only a few of the support roles useful to the resident. Institutions could add additional roles, such as a peer mentor, a community mentor, or a mentor in the local or state library association.

⑥ Defining the Resident's Role in the Organization

Defining the administrative structure of the residency can also help with defining the resident's role in the organization. Although some of this process is completed when gathering support for the residency (see chapter 3), clarifying the resident's position in the organizational chart can help their coworkers understand the resident's role in the organization. Figures 5.1 and 5.2 show two possible configurations of an organizational chart, highlighting the placement of a resident in an administration unit and in a library service department. Additionally, determining what kinds of committees the resident can serve on, what kinds of voting rights they have, what union they will be a member of, and what kinds of professional development funds they have access to is important to consider. If the residency is at an academic institution, will the resident be permitted to attend tenure proceedings? If it is at a public library, will the resident attend regular staff and departmental meetings?

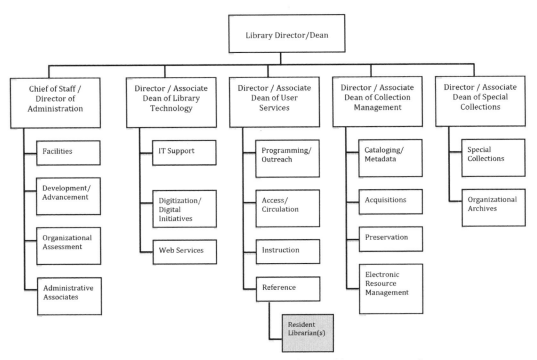

Figure 5.1. Sample organizational chart with resident in library service department

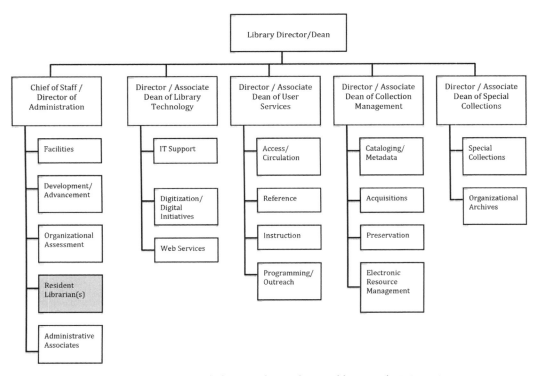

Figure 5.2. Sample organizational chart with resident in library administration

Determining the resources available to the resident for professional development is also important. If librarians at your institution receive funds to attend conferences or other professional development events, will the resident receive similar funds? Determining the answers to these questions during the planning stage of the residency makes it easier for the resident to understand the benefits and responsibilities they have in the organization.

Selection

It is January 2015. I'm just starting my last semester of the MSLIS at Pratt Institute. I am employed, in a way: I am a graduate assistant for a linked data research project at Pratt, and I am also a "genomer" (cataloger) for Artsy, an art startup. Even though it is only January, I decide to start figuring out my next move.

I'm not sure where I saw the job posting[1] for the Kress Fellowship in Art Librarianship at Yale. I waffled about applying. Thinking back on my decision to drop half of my dual master's program at Pratt, I figured that my chances of being chosen for such a competitive program were low. Still, I decided to apply as a way to practice what I imagined would be a pervasive background activity of my last semester of graduate school: writing cover letters and tweaking resumes.

To my incredible shock, I interviewed (the worst phone interview I'd ever had and my first full-day, in-person interview, which I felt great about) and in April found out that I'd been chosen to be the Kress Fellow. My dad, who is extremely supportive in general (he has all of my resumes and job offer letters taped to his office windows) and is also a Yale alum, was ecstatic that I'd finally ended up there (albeit through a side door).

The Fellowship

That first summer, getting settled. I live in East Rock, in between two Yale shuttle stops or a twenty-minute walk to campus. I walk to campus and enter the recently renovated space between Rudolf Hall (the Brutalist building designed by Paul Rudolph in 1963 that houses the School of Architecture) and the Loria Center (where the History of Art Department is). I greet Gloria, the security guard, and proceed to my office next to the circulation desk, which I share with Patty, the reference librarian. Patty was the previous Kress Fellow but stayed on. I've been asking her a lot of questions, especially about processing gift books, which I review for inclusion in the collection. I feel very lucky to share an office with her.

Later on in the year, I'm getting better at reference, through fast-paced, impromptu questions fielded at the circulation desk and referrals from colleagues, which I have more time to prepare for. I've got my spiel down about which databases and why, and how to facet and filter in our new library discovery interface. But today a graduate student has dropped by with an image of a drawing by Charles Moore that she's found on Tumblr. I discern that the minimal caption actually refers to the journal Art + Architecture, and suddenly we have a bridge between the world and the library. We are able to track down the print periodical in our stacks and look for books and articles. The student knocks on my office door shortly after to show me a book she's found with more drawings from the same series.

I walk to Bass Library and descend a hidden staircase at the edge of the lawn in front of Sterling, Yale's main library building. I enter an air conditioner–chilled classroom. I'm here for the Reference, Instruction, and Outreach committee meeting. I started going to fill in for a colleague, and then I kept going. There are librarians from other Yale libraries, like Sterling and the Center for Science and Social Science Information, some of whom have been here for many years. I share what's going on with our instruction sessions, and the group compares policies. I volunteer as co-coordinator of the group's journal club. Everyone welcomes my ideas, and I feel proud to represent the Arts Library.

Another day, I'm asked if I could cover a class visit to Arts Library Special Collections, and I leap at the chance. A photography professor is visiting with their undergraduate photography class to look at some MFA theses. I welcome everyone, helping the students sign in, put away their bags, and don white gloves. I instruct the students about how to handle photographic prints and remind them not to touch their faces and hair. The professor gives an intro to each artist, and I lay out the portfolios. The dark gray archival boxes, and the occasional cloth-bound box, come in all shapes and sizes: some portfolios cover the entire table in one unbroken surface; others contain photographs in a mix of sizes, leaving gaps where the blond tabletop shows through. We look at a range of work that the professor has chosen, from the 1970s to the last few years. I do a few more of these classes with the same professor, since I like them so much.

March 2016, the day of the Art + Feminism Wikipedia Edit-a-thon. It's the first time in a while that the library is open after hours, and the tray of sandwiches and other snacks are even more of a rarity (we have a no food policy). People start to arrive and the circulation desk is abuzz as we register people for their Wikipedia accounts on two laptops; I've trained a couple of our student workers and they're doing great. A few people who are experienced editors cross over from the circulation desk area to the paprika-carpeted stacks, settling at the tables lining the edges. My supervisor and mentors from the Arts Library are there, helping out or participating themselves. The curatorial fellow from the Yale Art Gallery who collaborated with us arrives. My colleague, Danielle, is setting up to give the training session in our library classroom. A group of undergraduate students gathers with their TA for History of the English Language. The TA and I have been working together to pull materials and make a list of relevant articles to improve. I don't actually end up editing anything because I'm running around, but it feels amazing that it's all actually happening after so many months of e-mailing and coordinating.

Fast forward to the 2018 ARLIS/NA conference, which is happening in New York City, where I've relocated. The Sunday before the conference starts, the Kress Foundation hosts a gathering to celebrate the twentieth anniversary of the fellowship. Over wine and tiny hors d'oeuvres, I chat with Kress Fellows and supervisors past and present. Some I am friends with, others I know from professional organizations, and yet another I had met at a workshop but not realized he was a past fellow. I meet one of the early fellows, who now directs an art library, and am a little starstruck: one of my tasks had been to see if we could migrate an exhibition website she had created to Omeka, and later on I'd found material she'd added to the book arts ephemera collection I was processing as another one of my fellowship projects. I feel a sense of warm connection being in a room with others who share experiences and hearing about what they have built in subsequent years; even though not much time has passed since my fellowship, I feel like I have already started building on the experience myself.

Reflection

Whenever I talk to people about my Kress Fellowship, I gush that it was how an internship is supposed to be: I got to do the perfect mix of day-to-day work and time to do my own projects. It really felt like it was designed to build my skills—not just one skill but a rounded skill set. I also had frequent meetings with all of the arts librarians I worked with. They were invested in my work, and it felt to me like I had not just one mentor but many.

My comments about the fellowship being "the perfect internship" should be seen in the context of library and arts internships more broadly. These are too often unpaid or are low-paying jobs disguised as internships. In contrast, my fellowship was designed to help me gain skills, and I also felt valued as a colleague by my mentors and other librarians at Yale. Another problem is that often professional development experiences like residencies and internships are most accessible to those with privilege. I am a white woman from a wealthy background; I have savings and have been able to afford to not work or to work for little money. I didn't have to have a full-time job while I was pursuing my MSLIS; I was able to dabble in different areas of interest with a graduate assistantship and a freelance job and a couple of unpaid volunteer gigs. Additionally, my fellowship year was one of transition; previously, the fellowship had been eight months, while mine was a twelve-month appointment. However, the salary did not increase by much. I ended up dipping into savings or getting help from my parents to afford my one-bedroom apartment and car. These amenities made me comfortable and made my year easier than it would have been if I'd had to worry about my budget or live with a roommate I didn't know. As I mention in my story, I also had help moving, which can be a costly and difficult process.

To build on how privilege impacts library work and residencies, race and class factor into experiences of belonging and inclusion. Both my white grandfather and father attended Yale; culturally, it was a place I had no trouble imagining I belonged. This was put into stark relief when my partner came to visit me on weekends; as a Dominican American, he did not feel as comfortable. Even coming from my background, when I was applying for the fellowship, I assumed it was too prestigious for me. This points to the risk that prospective library residents may not think they can successfully be chosen and then actually successfully participate.

Another point I think my stories bring up is the temporary nature of residencies and fellowships. When I planned events like the edit-a-thon, worked with the same professor for class visits, or attended committee meetings, I was trying to forge lasting work relationships with colleagues in the library and beyond. I am grateful that my fellowship allowed me to practice building these kinds of connections, even if there was an element of wistfulness that I wouldn't be able to see them through. Somewhat relatedly, outside of work I didn't try to put down social roots; I had a few friends, but I knew I'd be leaving at the close of the year and had a partner back in New York. For me, the year was a welcome respite from living in New York City, but I could easily imagine that being in a place temporarily could have been difficult psychologically.

In my last story, I talk about attending a reception for current and past fellows. This was a formal manifestation of the informal network that has existed among fellows. Though I was lucky to overlap with my predecessor, normally Kress Fellows do not work together. The reception event brought home for me that the network of colleagues who have done the same fellowship/residency is of great potential benefit, if those connections are nurtured and promoted by the institutions supporting the program. I've also been able to keep in touch with others I worked with during my fellowship year; though we aren't working together anymore, there is an enduring professional network.

Key Points

- Understanding the resident's position in the organization is essential to providing clarity about the benefits and responsibilities of the position.
- Finding people to serve as a residency coordinator, a supervisor, a project or area advisor, and a mentor helps to build a strong support network for the resident before they come to the institution.
- Determining the resident's role in the organization, as well as rights and responsibilities, is important for helping the resident and colleagues understand where they fit in the organization.

Note

1. Yale University Library, "Kress Fellowship 2015/2016 Job Description," *Yale University Library Subject Guides*, December 4, 2014, web.archive.org/web/20141204081916/https://guides .library.yale.edu/KressFellowship.

Reference

Yale University Library. "Kress Fellowship 2015/2016 Job Description." *Yale University Library Subject Guides*, December 4, 2014. web.archive.org/web/20141204081916/https://guides .library.yale.edu/KressFellowship.

Recruiting and Hiring for the Residency

ONCE THE INSTITUTION HAS DEVELOPED the administrative and programmatic structure for the residency, it is time to plan to bring a resident into the institution. Although recruiting and hiring can be challenging, planning ahead and applying strategic techniques can simplify the process. This chapter will describe key elements of recruitment and hiring, including developing a timeline, creating and posting the position description, reviewing applications, interviewing candidates, and hiring strong candidates.

The recruitment and hiring process is an important time to build a relationship between the organization and residency candidates. All of the candidates who review the recruitment materials or participate in interviews build an impression of the library through their interactions, even if they choose not to take a position or are not offered one. Thus, the recruitment process is an important opportunity to focus on portraying the institution's strengths and core commitments in a way that helps candidates decide whether they could envision themselves working there. For the library, recruitment and hiring processes offer a chance to find a candidate that meets the required qualifications for the residency and can contribute to the institution's growth over time. Since so much rides on finding a mutually beneficial relationship between the candidate and the institution, spending adequate time to recruit an excellent pool of candidates and hire a resident who is a good fit for the institution is important. Table 6.1 shows an example timeline for a resident library search.

⑥ Developing a Timeline

One of the first steps in planning the recruitment and hiring process is to develop a timeline for each step that enables the institution to hire the resident in time for an expected start date. Recruitment and hiring often includes several stages, including:

- defining the business need and required competencies,
- convening the search committee,
- developing the job description,
- posting the position and engaging in other recruitment activities,
- reviewing applications,
- scheduling and completing interviews, and
- hiring a candidate.

Table 6.1. Sample Resident Librarian Search Timeline

December 16	Job posted
Jan. 15	Search committee meets to review timeline. Phone interview questions and the topic for a public presentation are determined.
Jan. 24–28	Midwinter meeting of the American Library Association. Attending committee members are to distribute materials and encourage applicants to apply.
February 17	Search Committee meets for orientation and introduction to the search—20–30 minutes with the Office for Equal Opportunity, followed by application review to determine who will be asked for phone interviews.
March 2–3	Skype interviews will be conducted. The average time per interview is 30 minutes, with a 15-minute break in between.
March 4	The Search Committee will meet to review the Skype interviews and compare ranking sheets and notes.
April 6–17	In-person interviews. The Search Committee will meet with each candidate twice, once at the beginning of each interview and once at the end for a wrap-up session.
April 17	Feedback about candidates is due from campus members who watched the public presentation or met with the candidate.
April 20	Search Committee meets and makes a final list highlighting the candidate's skills and attributes, as well as areas for growth.
April 29	Librarian vote and approval. The Dean must call this meeting and make the final approval.
Beginning of May	Additional administrative proposals gained and job offered to candidate.

◎ Defining the Business Need and Required Competencies

Although the resident has a term-limited position that focuses on professional development, the organization likely has specific business needs they expect the resident to meet, such as being able to support short-term projects and regular operational services that require additional staffing. This is an opportunity to define what knowledge, skills, or abilities the resident needs to have coming into the position. For instance, it is common to require that applicants complete a master's in library science (MLS) or equivalent degree by the time the position starts. This is also a good opportunity to decide where the resident best fits in the organizational hierarchy, if you have not completed this step already.

◎ Convening the Search Committee

The next step in the process is to convene the search committee. Although many institutions have standard requirements about how search committees are formed, the following people should be included at minimum:

- the residency coordinator,
- the residency supervisor,
- representatives from at least one of the departments where the resident will work, and
- an administrator or member of the human resources department.

It is also worth considering drawing search committee members from library working groups, such as diversity and inclusion committees. Membership on search committees for new residents should rotate regularly to bring in new people.

◎ Creating the Position Description

In addition to forming the search committee, another major step to take is developing a position description, using the business needs and required competencies list developed in step 1 as a guide. Other key elements of the posting, such as position outcomes, will come directly from the desired outcomes identified in chapter 4. The position description is also the appropriate place to list any requirements for the position, such as a master's degree in library science or equivalent. The position description should also share or link candidates to more information about the institution, including the mission statement and strategic plan. ARL SPEC Kit 44, Talent Management (2014) reflects that survey respondents from ARL institutions find the following emphases most successful in recruitment:

- benefits packages,
- professional development opportunities,
- professional responsibilities,
- work environment, and
- institutional reputation.[1]

Highlighting the benefits that the resident will have (including medical and dental coverage), the professional development opportunities available, the kinds of professional skills and responsibilities they will develop, the positive aspects of the work environment, and the institutional reputation in the job description may encourage candidates to consider your institution in detail.

The job description should also include information about your community and local environs. Wheeler notes:

> In addition to presenting information that may be common knowledge (i.e., the South enjoys mild winters; the Midwest enjoys a low cost of living), addressing common misconceptions will go a long way toward selling your location. These may include the idea that small towns lack diversity and cultural events or that big cities suffer from long commutes and a high cost of living. Neither of these characterizations is helpful to recruiting and can be quickly dispelled with some elaboration, such as "small college town X enjoys a diverse population and hosts a wide variety of annual cultural events, including a world-class opera and classical music performances," or "big city Y has a number of unique and affordable neighborhoods within the city and enjoys a low cost of living compared to other cities its size." These statements can influence candidates who are strongly motivated by geographical considerations to apply.[2]

The position description is another important opportunity to consider principles related to diversity and inclusion. Many rote statements encouraging women and minorities to apply to positions may seem insincere; instead, as Buller advises, "far more useful would be a statement that explains why the institution is committed to diversity or that invites the applicant to discuss a commitment to diversity in his or her application."[3] These statements give your institution an opportunity to state in its own words its commitment to diversity.

**EXAMPLE DIVERSITY AND INCLUSION
STATEMENT FROM COLUMBIA UNIVERSITY**

Columbia University is an affirmative action, equal opportunity employer. The University is dedicated to the goal of building a culturally diverse and pluralistic faculty and staff committed to teaching and working in a diverse environment and strongly encourages applications from women, minorities, individuals with disabilities, and veterans.[4]

Posting the Position Description

Once the position is ready to post, the next step is to determine where to post it. There are multiple job boards for information science and library-related jobs, as well as listservs available through professional associations that target library job seekers. Many of these outlets target different audiences and have different length and formatting requirements, so it may be useful to develop a shortened version of the position description. When considering places to post the position, consider sharing it directly with institutions graduating a diverse class or with listservs or conference pages for underrepresented groups.

It may take a little while for the position posting to go public, so leave a week or more in the timeline for the job to actually go up. Job postings in many institutions stay open for six to eight weeks. During this time, your human resources department may receive questions from applicants about when they can expect to hear back on the position. At this point, it can be helpful to share the date when applications will be reviewed and when you expect to hire for the position. If you are not using an online application system, it is also important to send an e-mail or letter letting applicants know that their application has been received.

BIAS IN HIRING

Scientists Mahzarin Banaji and Anthony Greenwald have done a significant amount of work on "blind spots," or "ingrained habits of thought that lead to errors in how we perceive, remember, reason, and make decisions."[5] The habits of thought, also called implicit biases, stem from our brain's desire to make quick decisions based on our mental schemas, which tend to favor people that are "like us."[6] For example, two researchers submitted resumes to multiple positions, varying them by including one with a name suggesting an African American identity and another with a name suggesting a White American identity. Even though the qualifications were the same, the African American name received a call back 6.45 percent of the time, compared to 9.65 percent of the time for White name. These suggestions indicate that implicit bias may play a strong role in hiring.[7]

In order to mitigate some of the harms of implicit bias, some of the following strategies might be useful:

- Have the same interview questions for every candidate.
- Avoid "selective helpfulness," or the tendency to give extra help to people in privileged categories; one major way to do this is to rank candidates on the basis of their qualifications instead of deciding who to invite by using subjective judgements.[8]
- Focus on the information you have about the candidate from the resume and job interviews. Do not look for additional information about them on Facebook or the Internet.

Although implicit bias is impossible to erase completely, standardizing hiring and review procedures can enable search committees to function more effectively.

Gathering and Reviewing Applications

The next step is to review the applications. At the reviewing stage, it is important to develop a strategy that allows the search committee to compare candidates' knowledge, skills, and abilities in fair and equitable ways. Keeping in mind that implicit bias can appear in all parts of the search process, it's important to scrutinize the criteria for judging applications, many of which are laden with assumptions about the resources that applicants have at their disposal. April Hathcock identifies a number of these possible assumptions. These include: the expectation of recommendation letters, which assumes that applicants have been able to build close relationships with people in power in their early career; volunteer experience, which requires substantial financial resources; and the ability to describe how past work experience is relevant to library work, which can require a level of access to professional mentoring that may not be realistic for everyone.[9] While the search committee may not have the wherewithal to change application requirements, it does have the wherewithal to interrogate the assumptions behind how the applications are evaluated. A common strategy for search committees is to rank how each candidate meets each minimum and preferred qualification in the job description. If the committee chooses this strategy, it's important to build a shared and equitable understanding of what constitutes having met a particular qualification; this should include considering how applicants may meet qualifications in ways outside the norms of what committee members may be used to seeing in "successful applications" for positions requiring or preferring several years of experience. This process can reward the committee with a strong candidate pool and build the basis for a rigorous review that makes it easier to choose who to invite for a phone or electronic interview.

⑥ Planning and Conducting Interviews

The next step is to plan for and conduct interviews. Many institutions interview a certain percentage of applicants via telephone during the first round, followed by inviting three candidates for in-person interviews. The phone or video interviews are a great opportunity to get more information about why the candidate is interested in the position and how well their experiences match up with the required and preferred qualifications for the job. Most phone interviews are short, approximately thirty minutes or so, which often leaves enough time for around five questions. It is also a good idea to leave time at the end for the candidate to ask questions.

Since the time period for the search committee to ask questions is short, questions during this portion of the process should focus on allowing the candidate to share more

---

SAMPLE TELEPHONE INTERVIEW QUESTIONS

1. Tell us about how this position fits with your professional goals.
2. During the first year, the resident will rotate through the library's four departments: Research and User Services, Special Collections, Information Technology and Digital Library Services, and Collections and Scholarly Resources and Collections. Which department are you most interested in and why?
3. Tell us about a time when you received constructive criticism from a colleague or supervisor. How did you use the feedback to improve your performance?
4. Tell us about a time when you really succeeded at working independently and then really succeeded in working as a member of a team. What are your strengths in each of those cases?
5. What questions do you have for us?

information about how they meet the qualifications for the position without requiring them to repeat the information in the application. The phone interview is a great opportunity, for instance, to ask for specific examples of how the resident has demonstrated important skills, such as staying abreast of trends in the profession. In order to enhance efficiency, it may be useful to give the residency candidates the questions ahead of time. While many may view this practice as lowering an unspoken bar in the interview process, it has multiple benefits. It provides the candidate (who is, after all, early-career as a librarian) with an opportunity to decode and reflect on what the search committee is attempting to evaluate or measure in each question and to provide thoughtful and relevant responses. This saves time that the candidate might otherwise spend struggling to answer questions in as many different ways as possible. The practice of providing questions beforehand may also send a welcoming and positive message that candidates may appreciate in a prospective employer—that the organization's culture is open and transparent and invests in the success of its employees. Although some view the provision of phone interview questions as "scripting" the interview, there generally remains an entire in-person interview, which provides many opportunities for observing how final candidates "think on their feet."

During these interviews, it helps to develop a standardized format for each interview, including a greeting, introduction of the search members, brief description of the position, and reminder of how long the interview is planned to last. Although asking follow-up questions based on candidates' remarks is appropriate, questions should remain the same for each candidate in order to avoid receiving uneven information about the candidates. When possible, it is best for all of the search committee members to take notes in order to have a complete picture of the candidates' responses. After the group has reviewed the responses, they can then complete a second evaluation using the evaluation system they used when reading the applications.

Assuming that your interview process is multi-stage, the next step will be to meet with the search committee to decide who should be invited to an in-person interview. If all of your members have evaluated the candidates, evaluations should be pooled together to make this decision. In some institutions, a ranking system is used at this stage, which may make it a relatively easy computational decision. However, keep in mind that ranking at this stage often relies on many implicit biases common to the library profession (see above), which may be counter to the search committee's purposes, particularly if your residency is a diversity residency. If possible, it is best to invite at least three candidates. Although some institutions may invite only one or two candidates, this leaves relatively little working room if the interviews do not conclude with any recommendation to hire or if the candidate(s) decline the position. Three or so candidates provides the institution with multiple options to consider.

If the search committee plans to have the candidate offer a scholarly presentation or teach a sample class, it is appropriate to let them know the topic they should prepare for when making the invitation for an in-person interview. Some institutions decide to notify the candidates that they will need to present but avoid giving the presentation topic to each candidate until a set number of days before the interview in order to ensure that no candidate has more time to prepare than another. Some institutions may choose not to ask residency candidates to present at all. There may be multiple valid arguments for this choice. Some institutions may not ask candidates for any position to present. Others may choose specifically not to require candidates for the residency to present, in the spirit of providing an entry-level interview for an entry-level position. The practice of requiring a scholarly presentation as part of an interview is often laden with an expectation that the candidate is already above the entry level as a scholar and a practitioner. Whether or not your organization chooses to require candidates for the residency to present, be aware of how differences between the resident's interview process and the interview process of candidates for other positions will impact their colleagues' perceptions of them when they arrive. If the presentation is the only "public" time in the interview at which staff and community members may observe or have input into the search, be sure to build another public segment into the in-person interview.

As soon as possible, it is also considerate to send the candidate a copy of the interview schedule so that they have some sense of what to expect for the interview day. Interview schedules may include times and locations for:

- dinner the night before (most common in academic interviews);
- arrival and greeting on the day of the interview;
- tour of the library;
- panel interview with the search committee;
- presentation, meet and greet, or other "public" time;
- lunch;
- interview or meeting with members of the resident's unit or desired units of rotation;
- meeting with the library director or dean; and
- administrative paperwork, particularly for travel reimbursement.

Where possible, interview schedules should also be accompanied by other necessary details, such as directions to the library, locations for parking, and how the candidate is expected to book travel and be reimbursed if they are coming from outside the local area. Many interviews involve taking the candidate to dinner the night before, followed by meetings with the search committee, other library employees, and library administrators. If the residency interviews will also include a public presentation, this should also be built into the interview planning process.

During the planning stages, the search committee should develop a standard list of questions to ask the candidate. When developing questions, it can be helpful to focus on questions that elicit specific examples of how the candidate's knowledge, skills, and abilities fit the needs of the residency position. Since candidates for a residency position may not have a lot of work experience, questions should allow candidates to respond with examples from their time in school when possible. It may also be helpful to ask questions about the candidate's past work and relationships since research and common wisdom suggest that past behavior is a predictor of future behavior.[10] Once interviews are complete, be clear with the candidates about when they can expect to hear an update. Since many candidates apply for multiple positions, being clear about the timeline for the position is important.[11] Include some leeway in this time period, especially if building and extending an offer involves obtaining multiple levels of approval.

Table 6.2. Sample Agenda for Resident Librarian Candidate Interviews

NIGHT BEFORE:	
5:15p	One of us will meet the candidate at the hotel to drive to dinner
5:30–7:30p	Dinner (two or three people)
DAY OF :	
8:30a	One search committee member picks up candidate from hotel, brings to library
9:00–10:00a	Search committee meets with candidate
10:00–10:30a	Break and setup for presentation (if required)
10:30–11:30a	Presentation followed by Q&A and light reception
11:30a–12:00p	Candidate meeting with dean of the library
12:00–1:00p	Lunch meeting with resident librarian supervisor
1:00–2:00p	Tour
2:00–3:00p	Meet with the library faculty
3:00–3:15p	Break
3:15–4:00p	Wrap up with search committee

SAMPLE IN-PERSON INTERVIEW QUESTIONS

1. Tell us why you are interested in the resident librarian position. How will participating help you meet your professional goals?
2. In this position, you would be working with a number of different people, each of whom will give you feedback. Imagine that you received feedback that you did not agree with. Has this ever happened to you? How did you handle it? What strategies would you use to handle it in this position?
3. Describe a project you completed where you were a member of a team. What role did you play? What did you find easy about working in a group and what did you find more challenging?
4. This position often works with diverse populations of people. Can you give us an example of your experience working with a diverse group of people?
5. Describe a project or activity in which you took a major leadership role. What was the project? How did you demonstrate leadership? How would you apply those characteristics in this position?
6. Part of the job description says: use of multiple technologies to advance library goals. Potential activities include the creation and maintenance of online teaching and learning tools; assessment; development and maintenance of print, multimedia, and digital library collections; or maintenance and development of the library's web presence and discovery tools. Which of these do you feel most ready to work on and which do you expect to have the greatest learning curve?

7. Tell us about your prior work experience. What would be similar and what would be different in this position?
8. A part of this position will be outreach to the university community. What ideas and/or skills do you have to offer in this endeavor?
9. If you had control over creating the ideal work environment for you, what would it be like? What would the people that you work with be like?
10. Imagine that you are offered the job and accept. What would you do during the first month to get up to speed?
11. What questions do you have for us?

Making an Offer

During the interviews, all of the search committee members should take notes about the candidates' responses. Then, when the search committee meets to rank the candidates, they rely on what they have written down rather than memory. Before the ranking, campus members should be given ample time to share feedback about the candidates. If the feedback is relevant to the position, it should be considered when the committee meets. When you are ready to make the offer, it may be helpful to share with the candidate another copy of the job description as well as any onboarding plans you have already made; this can help to overcome the challenge of candidates who withdraw from a position after obtaining it.[12]

Although developing a detailed hiring plan and process takes a good deal of time, investing the effort before beginning the search can simplify the process. During the search, committee members are often quite busy, and having a clear plan makes it easier to avoid mishaps. In many cases, residency candidates may also be anxious or uncertain about the process; providing them with as much information as possible can help them worry less about logistics and focus more on communicating with the search committee and their potential colleagues.

Key Points

- Be aware of the potential for bias throughout the hiring process and take steps to ameliorate it as much as possible.
- Standardize the hiring process in order to help prevent bias.
- Develop an adequate timeline to encompass all of the parts of the hiring process.
- Let the resident candidates know when they can expect to hear from your institution.

Notes

1. Meredith A. Taylor and Elida Lee, *SPEC Kit 344: Talent Management* (Washington, D.C.: Association of College and Research Libraries, 2014), 11.

2. Ronald E. Wheeler, Nancy P. Johnson, and Terrance K. Manion, "Choosing the Top Candidate: Best Practices in Academic Law Library Hiring," *Law Library Journal* 100, no. 1 (Winter 2008): 120.

3. Jeffrey L. Buller, *Best Practices for Faculty Search Committees: How to Review Applications and Interview Candidates* (San Francisco, Cal.: Jossey-Bass, 2017), 20.

4. Buller, *Best Practices for Faculty Search Committees.*

5. Mahzarin R. Banaji and Anthony G. Greenwald, *Blindspot: Hidden Biases of Good People* (New York: Delacorte Press, 2013), 4.

6. Ibid., 9.

7. Marianne Bertrand and Sendhil Mullainathan, "Are Emily and Greg More Employable Than Lakisha and Jamal? A Field Experiment on Labor Market Discrimination," *American Economic Review* 94, no. 4 (2004): 997.

8. Banaji and Greenwald, *Blindspot*, 160.

9. April Hathcock, "White Librarianship in Blackface: Diversity Initiatives in LIS," *In the Library with the Lead Pipe*, October 7, 2015, paras. 10–11, www.inthelibrarywiththeleadpipe.org/2015/lis-diversity/.

10. Diane Arthur, *Recruiting, Interviewing, Selecting & Orienting New Employees*, 5th ed. (New York: AMACOM, American Management Association, 2012).

11. Armin Trost, *Talent Relationship Management: Competitive Recruiting Strategies in Times of Talent Shortage* (New York: Springer Science & Business, 2014), 109.

12. Ibid., 120.

References

Arthur, Diane. *Recruiting, Interviewing, Selecting & Orienting New Employees.* 5th ed. New York: AMACOM, American Management Association, 2012.

Banaji, Mahzarin R., and Anthony G. Greenwald. *Blindspot: Hidden Biases of Good People.* New York: Delacorte Press, 2013.

Bertrand, Marianne, and Sendhil Mullainathan. "Are Emily and Greg More Employable Than Lakisha and Jamal? A Field Experiment on Labor Market Discrimination." *American Economic Review* 94, no. 4 (2004): 991–1013.

Buller, Jeffrey L. *Best Practices for Faculty Search Committees: How to Review Applications and Interview Candidates.* San Francisco, Cal.: Jossey-Bass, 2017.

Hathcock, April. "White Librarianship in Blackface: Diversity Initiatives in LIS." *In the Library with the Lead Pipe*, October 7, 2015. www.inthelibrarywiththeleadpipe.org/2015/lis-diversity/.

Taylor, Meredith A., and Elida Lee. *SPEC Kit 344: Talent Management.* Washington, D.C.: Association of College and Research Libraries, 2014.

Trost, Armin. *Talent Relationship Management: Competitive Recruiting Strategies in Times of Talent Shortage.* New York: Springer Science & Business, 2014.

Wheeler, Ronald E., Nancy P. Johnson, and Terrance K. Manion. "Choosing the Top Candidate: Best Practices in Academic Law Library Hiring." *Law Library Journal* 100, no. 1 (Winter 2008): 117–36.

Onboarding
Setting the Stage

THE START OF ANY NEW STAFF MEMBER'S TENURE is an important time. In most organizations, new staff members begin with some form of "onboarding," which is the process by which new employees are introduced to the organization, its work culture, and its mission and values. Much of the tone of new staff members' supervisory, departmental, and administrative relationships is struck in this period.[1] Significantly, many onboarding programs encompass not just the first few weeks after a new staff member's arrival but also much of the new staff member's acculturation to the workplace, often the first six months to two years.[2] Acculturation, or the process of learning about and adapting to a new culture,[3] is important for new employees' success; it is a process that can be facilitated but not rushed. This is particularly true in residency programs, most of which aim to support early-career librarians in navigating the library profession or entering into work in your library or archive type. Therefore, it is wise to keep in mind that onboarding may occupy a relatively high portion of the resident's time at the institution, and as such, it should be planned carefully. Since support for early-career professionals is a major goal in many residency programs, it is important to design it into the onboarding process, starting before the resident begins.

The onboarding process for new residents often begins well before their arrival; it is theorized that a thoroughly planned onboarding process reinforces a mutual belief that the organization and the new employee are good fits for one another.[4] Substantial existing literature shows that residents' experiences are highly influenced by indications of the extent to which program coordinators and library administrators educate the entire organization on what the residency is, why it was established, who the residents are, and what can be expected of the residents. Alston's research[5] particularly draws a significant correlation between residents' general rating of quality in their programs and their perception of the effort that coordinators and administrators make in garnering support for the residency from other library personnel. To that end, it is significant to build as much buy-in and anticipation of the residency program as possible; setting the stage for a first resident is a major point at which to do so.

If the concept of a residency program is new to the organization, staff across the entire library organization may have questions. This creates an opportunity to build upon initial information you already disseminated about the program and communicate to the entire organization about it and what to expect. Brewer suggested in a 2001 article[6] that coordinators use staff newsletters to communicate information about the residency program to all library personnel; it stands to reason that other broad channels of internal staff communication may also work well. These may include all-staff listservs, all-staff or departmental meetings, and internal communication applications. Through these, you can announce the filling of the new position and reiterate its programmatic nature (if your residency will be a sustained program) and its purpose within the library. At this point, you may also wish to emphasize that the program is not a typical contract or project position but plays a strategic role within the organization, and many individuals across the organization may be called upon to work with resident(s) in some capacity. Communicating about the residency program and about new residents through these channels is particularly important if the residency is rotational and staff members in the expected rotation areas have not had a chance to learn about or interact with potential residents during the interview process.

This is a point at which all of the stakeholders you identified while building support for the program (see chapter 3), particularly individuals and teams who will work with or mentor the resident, should be made well aware of the resident's imminent arrival. You should definitively secure commitment of participation from these direct players as far ahead of residents' arrival as possible and include them in the planning process for orientations. These players also need to be given guidelines on their roles in the onboarding process, as far before the resident's arrival as possible. This allows time to those individuals and groups for their own internal planning to include the resident in operational work and to identify projects that the resident may work on.

Many residency programs incorporate individual residents' interests and choices and therefore may need to wait until final candidates are identified in order to do this, making the time frame between solidifying stakeholders and the resident's arrival quite short. This is where the foundational work that you already laid of building support for the program prior to recruitment comes in handy (see chapter 3). It is much easier to build upon a foundation of earlier communications about the program, sent to the entire library organization, than to try to lay that foundation and communicate new roles and expectations mere weeks before the resident's arrival.

ⓖ Pre-arrival Communication with Residents

Most onboarding programs aim, in part, to provide opportunities for new employees to learn about social aspects of the organization and facilitate new employees' ability to perform all aspects of their jobs as quickly as possible. Therefore, communicating with the resident prior to the start date as part of the onboarding process may be helpful. Not every institution's human resources practice or policy allows this, but if you are able to do so, it can provide many opportunities.

Klein, Pollin, and Sutton note that the amount of information to be communicated to a new employee is best provided in chunks over time rather than all at once, to allow the new employee to digest and apply the information and avoid information overload.[7] Communication prior to a new employee's start date can be an opportunity to begin doing this; Graybill et al. conducted a study of ACRL libraries' onboarding practices indicating that four of seventeen libraries engaged in this practice by 2013.[8]

In communicating with incoming residents between their hire date and start date, it may be helpful to establish what area or department they will start in and who will oversee their everyday work in that area, if those aspects of the residency are not fixed. Opening communication during this time also creates an opportunity to support the residents and find out about any needs they may have that may impact their onboarding. For example, if the resident is relocating for the residency and has no personal connections in the area, it could be helpful to check in and ask if they need help or advice on where and how to find housing in the area. Because many residents are very early in their library careers, and because the general trend of high student debt continues to affect many early-career professionals, some residents may not have achieved the financial security to relocate without substantial difficulty. With this in mind, it may be helpful to provide payroll information; see the "Financial Considerations" section below for further details. Finally, opening communication with the resident prior to their arrival allows you to provide thorough instructions for first-day arrival, including timing, specific location within the library of arrival or first meeting, parking or public transportation nearby, lunch options in the vicinity, and so on.

ⓖ Communicating with Direct Players

In addition to the general communication with all staff about the residency program, direct players in the program will need specific details about their roles. This is particularly true if their roles within the residency program differ from their usual roles in the organization. It is worth noting that many residents build up their resumes by building and working on significant projects, even in departments that do not ordinarily operate through project cycles; project management may be a new role for many new resident supervisors.

Clearly communicating about and internally documenting all involved roles is particularly important because it is not always simple, or even possible, to document the relationship of all mentors or rotational supervisors in systematic or openly accountable ways, such as through organizational charts or within staff evaluation systems. For example, many rotational residencies place the resident within the administrative unit on the organizational chart (see figure 5.2), leaving any reporting relationships with hosting department supervisors undocumented. This trend is fairly understandable, given that residents may move across departments over time, as in rotational residencies, or the hosting unit of the residency may change as individual residents come and go based on staffing needs or residents' interests. However, coordinators and administrators should take some care early on to clearly explain roles and expectations of personnel who will work directly with residents. Chapter 5 describes some examples of the roles that personnel may need to fill, as well as some of the typical responsibilities related to each role.

Of course, once the residents start, they, too, should be informed of which types of issues or questions will be handled by a departmental supervisor, as opposed to a coordinator or administrator, and vice versa, as part of a library orientation (see chapter 8). However, the weight of knowing who plays what roles should not fall mainly on the resident, who, after all, has neither an experience of the organizational culture nor an experience of the residency program specifically. If guidelines are clearly defined to all direct players prior to the resident's arrival, they are more likely to be prepared to play their new roles and support the resident on arrival, which in turn allows the resident to focus on navigating their own role.

It may be inevitable when a new resident arrives, particularly if they are the first resident for your library, that their colleagues will come to them with questions regarding the term-limited nature of the position, their professional background, and their organizational role. However, being questioned excessively in this vein can send a tacit message to the resident that they are not expected within the organization and their role is not important enough to be well understood by their colleagues. This can factor strongly into low morale experiences for residents,[9] which in turn can lead to negative mental and physical health impacts, lowered interest and engagement in professional development, and negative outlooks on LIS as a career.[10] Thus, it is extremely important to communicate expectations, guidelines, and roles prior to residents' arrival. This can help to foster a sense of being expected and prepared for by colleagues, having meaningful roles to play, and having responsibilities that are equal to their capabilities and qualifications.

Area Advisors

If the resident will have day-to-day, departmental, or "on-site" supervisors, those supervisors should clearly know the expectations of supervising a resident. As noted in chapter 5, this includes supporting the resident's development of knowledge, skills, and abilities; supporting and monitoring the resident's day-to-day work; helping the resident connect with the rest of the work area; and more. At this point, you should also provide area supervisors or advisors with further details on the following:

- specific responsibilities in the resident's overall personnel evaluation,
- specific responsibilities in the assessment of the residency program,
- how their supervisory work with the resident will be evaluated,
- how the supervisory labor will be compensated, and
- time frame in which they will act as a resident's supervisor.

Area supervisors should also be informed of what they can expect from a resident and what the resident expects or needs from them. While this will largely take place through communication between the resident and the supervisor, residency program coordinators can help this process by facilitating early conversations between the supervisor and resident. Topics may include:

- skills that the resident already has;
- training that the resident may need for work that they will perform;
- training that the resident may desire to improve their skills or prospects;
- the time commitment that the resident will make to the work area;
- the time commitments that the resident will have beyond work for the hosting area (such as committee service, conference attendance, etc.); and
- key collaborators upon whom the resident's work may depend.

Residency Mentors

If the resident will have a formal or assigned mentor, it may be helpful to provide the mentor with some basic guidelines at this point. It is ordinary in mentorship programs to leave the tenor and specifics of the mentorship up to the mentor and the mentee, and the same will likely be true for mentorship within the residency program; however, the role of the mentor in the context of the program, among several other supportive roles, may not necessarily be clear. For example, the mentor may find it helpful to know:

- how their role supplements and differs from those of coordinators, administrators, and work supervisors (see chapter 5);
- potential time commitments required for their service;
- how their service is evaluated; and
- how their service is compensated.

Mentors may also find it helpful to hear examples of what they can do for residents that will not be covered by others, such as introducing the resident to collegial bodies within the library (including faculty committees, working groups, or continuing education committees); providing insights on or arranging orientation to their union, if they are a member of a union; or arranging tours of any branch libraries or other locations not covered in orientation tours.

⑥ Arrangements and Preparations

In the period between the resident's acceptance of the offer and their start date, you should make and finalize arrangements to ensure that the resident(s) will have all they need to perform their work, including arranging the resident's workstation and ensuring that they are included on all necessary listservs or communication channels. It may be helpful to the resident to receive a compiled handbook, especially one that is tailored specifically for the residency. Even if it is not yet a regular practice to provide an onboarding handbook to all new employees, it may be particularly needful for residents to receive one. This is because many residencies are built with a strategic component and are intended to have significant impact across the organization or with the intention that the resident should approach their work with a bird's-eye understanding of the organization. This being the case, their orientation may be broader or contain somewhat more information than is average for other positions, and it may help the resident to be able to go back to a broad document repository throughout their onboarding. See table 7.1 below for a worksheet to compile a resident's handbook.

Table 7.1. Worksheet for Compiling Resident Handbook

DOCUMENT	CREATION STATUS	ASSIGNED CREATOR	CREATION DEADLINE	HANDBOOK INTEGRATION STATUS
Welcome letter				
Orientation schedule				
Program mission & goals				
Rotation schedule or program structure outline				
Onboarding check-in meeting dates & talking points				
List of people the resident will be introduced to or set up meetings with during onboarding				
Standard staff training documents (ex: lists of core systems, collections, service policies to learn)				
Work log(s)				
Lists of regular staff meetings/ events, meetings directly related to the resident's work				
Prior residents' contact information (with prior residents' consent)				
Directory of library locations				
Maps of building, campus, and area				
Safety procedure				
Personnel evaluation outline or criteria				
Program evaluation outline or criteria				
Department list & synopses				
Professional development policies or guidelines				
Locations of significant policies & forms				
Organizational chart				
Information about employee assistance & EOE				
Position description				

Aside from readying informational materials for the resident, it is also important to build tools, such as orientation checklists, timelines and schedules, and copies of procedures and policies for all direct players in the resident's onboarding, including work supervisors, coordinators, and mentors. Although there will be significant overlap, differentiating tools and providing overviews that show where each person fits within the overall process will help it run smoothly. Checklists and timelines should include not just the first few weeks but also check-ins for significant milestones, such as thirty days, three months, six months, and twelve months. Table 7.2 provides an example of a project-specific timeline during the rotational year of a rotational residency.

Table 7.2. Sample Project or Rotation Timeline Based on a Timeline Created by Jessica Lydon, Temple University Libraries

Project begin date:	February 4
Project end date:	May 3
Project scope:	Process and digitize XYZ Collection (~10 linear feet)

Stage 1: Orientation & Training, February 4–February 15

1. Department introductions and tour
2. Review mutual goals and needs
3. Review project scope and timeline
4. Review regular meetings to attend
5. Read & review departmental policies, and training documents on processing, description, and digitization
6. Read & review materials from archival theory & practice reading list prepared by supervisor

Stage 2: Collection Survey & Accessioning, February 18–March 1

1. Resident conducts survey of the collection (collection is already identified)
2. Resident creates a collection survey document based on shared departmental survey template
3. Resident and supervisor review survey and make arrangements for any special preservation or housing needs

Stage 3: Collection Arrangement, March 4–March 15

1. Resident arranges collection
2. Resident re-houses collection as necessary
3. Resident creates folder-level inventory of collection
4. Resident performs research needed to understand the content and context of the collection
5. Resident and supervisor review inventory and progress weekly

Stage 4: Description & Access Tool Creation, March 18–April 5

1. Resident completes research on context of the collection
2. Resident creates finding aid and MARC record
3. Resident and supervisor review progress of description and access tools weekly

Stage 5: Digitization & Metadata, April 8–April 26

1. Resident performs scanning, versioning, and file-naming
2. Resident sets up or arranges setup of digital collection in digital asset management system
3. Resident uploads files
4. Resident inputs aggregate-level metadata (from finding aid)
5. Resident and supervisor review scanning progress twice weekly and adjust scale of digitization activities if needed

Stage 6: Finalization & Wrap-up, April 29–May 3

1. Resident finalizes and customizes digital collection
2. Resident and supervisor review any outstanding needs of the project
3. Resident and supervisor complete project/rotation report

⑨ Considerations and Potential Pitfalls

Building Support for Inclusion in Diversity Residencies

As stated in chapter 1, roughly two-thirds of the known active and sustained residency programs are identified as diversity residencies. They are usually designed to bring professionals of marginalized and underrepresented backgrounds to institutions that have identified a misalignment between the diversity of their served communities and their staff[11] and to the library profession, which has already identified broader misalignments between the composition of the general population and its own demographic composition.[12] While most do not explicitly state a concentration on racial and ethnic diversity, considerable LIS research demonstrates that the profession has long fallen short specifically on ensuring racial equity, diversity, and inclusion and that initiatives such as diversity residencies have a role to play in addressing the structural problems contributing to the overwhelming whiteness of the profession.[13]

It is commonly thought that diversity residencies, along with other diversity initiatives such as scholarships for minoritized students, effectively form a pipeline that naturally "brings diversity" into library institutions and into the library profession.[14] Yet, a multitude of research and observation shows that efforts to recruit for diversity are not effective by themselves. Rather, sustainable diversity requires interrogation and change of the existing culture that perpetuates the profession's homogeneity and inequity.

It may be helpful to think about what the resident has already gone through by the time they reach onboarding. This includes the application and hiring process, which are known to present barriers for many people with marginalized backgrounds in an early and vulnerable stage in their journeys into the profession (see chapter 6). In addition to the barriers that diversity residents face as candidates on job hunts, they inevitably face barriers and marginalization on the actual job as well. These may be individually actionable barriers, such as difficulties in the process and paperwork of disclosing a disability and requesting reasonable accommodations, or they may be systemic barriers that may take time and broad suites of action to address meaningfully, such as treatment of residents as "token" others.

Some examples of individual actions that can help to lower some barriers in the pre-arrival portion of onboarding include:

- facilitating reasonable accommodations requests, which generally involve a significant amount of paperwork;
- notifying the incoming resident of upcoming requirements between the offer date and the start date, especially those that may call for upfront fee payments, including drug tests or vaccinations;
- providing information about when to expect initiation into health insurance and payroll (see also "Financial Considerations" section); and
- ensuring that the resident is initiated into and introduced to all e-mail lists and groups that are relevant to their work and their professional librarian status.

There are also broader phenomena indicative of wide institutional and workplace cultural issues that present particular difficulties to diversity residents. While there are no singular actions that can mitigate these, it is important to believe and affirm residents when they confide experiences of these to you and to introduce incremental initiatives toward cultural change, including education and policy. These include:

- Microaggressions: A term coined by Chester M. Pierce,[15] this refers to verbal and behavioral cues in everyday interactions that intentionally or unintentionally denigrate marginalized groups of people. Many people embodying marginalized identities experience an accumulation of many microaggressions over the course of daily interactions. Rosalinda Hernandez Linares and Sojourna J. Cunningham frame this experience in library diversity residencies using Kristie A. Ford's terminology of "bodily misrecognition," and their research uncovers many ways in which diversity residents are pressured to perform "body management."[16] This refers to changing or stifling behaviors or modes of expression, often tied to cultural identity, in order to assimilate or to escape negative stereotyping.
- Vocational awe: This refers to a set of values and rhetoric that frame libraries as inherently good and beyond critique, underpinning many librarians' emotional investment in the profession. Coined by Fobazi Ettarh, this term names a toxic phenomenon that negatively affects many librarians by multiple means, including by positioning critique of the library profession or library workplaces as "unprofessional" and by pressuring many library workers to sacrifice healthy work-life balance for "love of the work."[17] This concept does not discourage passion for and investment in librarianship; it merely encourages critical and thoughtful use of rhetoric about new librarians' passion and enthusiasm.
- Tokenism: This refers to the practice of including a small number of minority individuals due to legal or social pressures, as well as its effects on those individuals. These effects include: isolation as cultural outsiders, high visibility, pressure to speak for an entire group of people, pressure to perform, restriction of power, and risk of burnout.[18]

With these factors in mind, residency coordinators and administrators should critically examine not only application requirements (see chapter 6) but also onboarding processes, to consider where they present barriers to the retention of diverse talent and work to mitigate them.

The onboarding planning and process should include consistent questioning of whether your internal expectations, such as what successful "socialization to the organizational culture" looks like or what constitutes "professional behavior," match the espoused desires to diversify. Questions to ask of each stage of the onboarding process include:

- Can this stage of the process more meaningfully bring the resident into the formal and informal mentoring networks in the workplace?
- What assumptions are made about the resident in this stage of the process? How will you verify whether these assumptions are correct, and what changes will you make if they are not?
- Are there mechanisms built in to ensure that the resident will have an equal balance of meaningful challenges and healthy work-life balance?
- How will you balance between advocating for the resident and ensuring that the resident retains the right to speak for themself?

As part of their preparations for onboarding a new resident, residency coordinators and administrators should both undergo and host diversity trainings to heighten their awareness of privilege, implicit bias, and dynamics of power and oppression. Even for programs that are not explicitly defined as recruiting underserved groups, such training is helpful. Pickens and Coren explicitly suggest that coordinators and administrators undergo diversity training in their 2017 article on building diversity residency programs.[19] Although many institutions already require new supervisors and managers to undergo basic training on "workplace civility" policies, it is suggested that diversity residency coordinators go a step further and seek deeper knowledge on the ways in which social oppression manifests in everyday dynamics and on mitigating the negative effects that residents incur in having been hired as "tokens." Additionally, by no means should efforts to support diversity residents stop at training, whether formal or informal. Training merely hones a critical lens by which to examine the various stages of onboarding and how well the process supports residents and improve upon it.

Financial Considerations

For a multitude of reasons, early-career professionals may have substantial financial stresses and considerations to take into account in accepting a residency. For example, many residents may bear significant student debt from undergraduate and graduate school. For some, the residency may be a first full-time job, or a first job in your institution type, and particularly, it may be the first position for which there is a tacit expectation that they will negotiate for their salaries. Some residents may live with disabilities, invisible or visible; some may have families to support; some may be coming in from a period of underemployment, unemployment, or employment without health benefits. Some residents may have several of these considerations, all of them, or entirely different considerations that play into their financial condition as they begin a residency.

Particularly for those who relocate, the costs of accepting a residency may be unexpectedly high, as most institutions, even those that provide relocation assistance, do not fully fund the relocation. Keep in mind that, in order to relocate, new employees need to cover not only the costs of moving their possessions and their person but also the costs of securing a place to live, which generally include a trip to the area to view housing options and the payment of a security deposit and first month's rent. It may sometimes require that the new employees pay for temporary living quarters, such as a hotel, at the start of their tenure, while they secure a more permanent living situation. It is worth noting that many landlords also require a credit check prior to approval of a lease and may impose additional upfront fees to individuals with credit scores below a certain threshold. In combination with other possible factors such as student debt, financial stress from underemployment or unemployment with no health benefits prior to the residency, and any number of other factors, this may leave the resident financially struggling for considerable time even after initiation into the payroll. For these reasons, though it may not be standard onboarding procedure or policy, we suggest that residents be provided with meaningful support in facing the financial burdens of accepting the residency. Meaningfully supporting a resident's financial needs may include:

- providing information for moving businesses that the organization works regularly with and/or has discounts with;
- providing information on available campus housing and housing support;

- providing timely information regarding the availability of salary advances and the process for obtaining one;
- providing payroll information, including frequency of pay and the timing of the resident's first paycheck;
- providing information about when insurance benefits will be available; and
- securing a comprehensive relocation package.

Why Should I Do All of This?

Setting the stage for a new resident's arrival, especially a first resident's arrival, can be a very involved process, requiring substantial time and resources that may be difficult to spare. You may be asking yourself whether every aspect, including the process of building buy-in across the organization, building explicit roles for a multitude of direct players, arranging for fair compensation for all direct players, providing pre-arrival support to the resident, and building a full handbook and schedule for the resident's onboarding, is necessary. Understandably, all of these steps can add up to a significant amount of over-head to prepare for and run a new residency, and this may feel somewhat overwhelming. However, all of them help to ensure a supportive and organized residency program and, most importantly, set up your residents for success.

As noted in chapter 2, residency programs hold enormous potential for major benefits to your library and for the profession. Residency programs often support major strategic goals in libraries' organizational plans. For example, residencies can act as a major means by which libraries gain staff members who work on significant and cutting-edge projects; diversity residencies can be part of a library's work on strategic goals related to building the organization's capacity to hire and retain diverse workers. Residency programs can thus be major initiatives through which an organization expresses what it values. As Oates points out in the autoethnography below, overcoming the barriers to creating the structures and material conditions of a well-conceived and supportive residency is one of the best ways of valuing all it brings to the organization.

KJV OR NIV? RESIDENT BIBLES/MANUALS ARE NOT OPTIONAL
by Evangela Q. Oates

Introduction

It is possible that residency programs in library and information sciences (LIS) were popular prior to 2005, but I do not remember seeing any announcements before applying to the University of New Mexico's University Libraries (UNM UL) Resident Program. In truth, I did not know they existed. The extent of my knowledge of the word *resident* was medically based, referring to training programs where new physicians receive their completion of medical school. It was not until I read the job description that I realized I could possibly get an entry-level position in an academic library. For me, this was very attractive as I had heard about the difficulties of getting into academic librarianship. So I applied for the position and was most happy to accept their offer. I should clarify that this Resident Program was not geared to hiring librarians from racial minoritized backgrounds, rather it sought to offer new librarians a way to enter the profession. However, both residents that preceded me were Native American, and the university is designated as a Hispanic Serving Institution.

My success as a resident can be attributed to several factors: intentional planning, mentorship, and organizational support. These areas are most important for coordinators, especially if they intend to have a successful program.

Intentional Planning

When I arrived on campus, I could tell there had been much anticipation and preparation for my position. The coordinator of the program spent a lot of time compiling a manual (I called it the "bible") that detailed my orientation to University Libraries (UL). This was crucial as I did not have to make assumptions; it clearly explained each department (staff, contact information, title, etc.), my rotation throughout departments, and what each department was responsible for. Even though my official title alluded to prominent duties in public services, I was allowed to choose projects from access, technical, systems, government documents, archives, and special collections. Looking back, I appreciate the inclusion of these areas as it gave me the opportunity to explore which parts of librarianship best suited my skills and interest.

I chose projects based on proposals that had been submitted to the coordinator. In order to get assistance on new or current projects, library faculty were asked to submit detailed proposals to the program coordinator. This was in response to feedback given by previous residents. I do not recall if they were given formal program assessments, but I did hear that their experience was not as positive due to lack of oversight and planning. With a new coordinator on board, many of these issues were corrected. The new system was developed as a way to ensure that residents were not exploited and to give a sense of agency (to the resident) as new faculty. Proposals required that specific outcomes, outputs, and deadlines were listed. My advice to coordinators is to consider the personality, seniority, and productiveness of the person submitting the proposal. Do *not* place a resident with someone who has a history of abuse, bullying, or poor performance. They should be invested in the success of the resident. Periodic check-ins should be required and if the project changes in any way, coordinators should be notified immediately as to share pertinent updates (staffing, resources, etc.).

Mentorship

The coordinator has become my mentor, and this relationship developed as a result of the Resident Program. In the beginning, we met weekly to talk about my adjustment to the region, university, culture, and position. I enjoyed having this time to be able to openly share my experiences (on campus and external) and solicit advice. Depending on one's lens, this could be considered micromanagement, but I never felt smothered by the frequency of our meetings, nor did I view them as a way to monitor my movements. I was fortunate that my coordinator genuinely cared about my integration into the department and the university. Eventually, our weekly meetings became bi-weekly meetings, until we ultimately decided that meeting every month was more than sufficient. Even though we modified our schedules, we never considered canceling our meetings as we understood they renewed a sense of importance regarding the basis for the Resident Program. On a few occasions, these meetings helped uncover untruthful allegations that in many cases could have influenced my performance evaluation. In one scenario, someone had reported that I was not good at reference. This is not what I wanted to hear! As a new librarian, I was a bit self-conscious about my preparedness at the reference desk, so it did not help to hear that another librarian thought I was bad at it. I remember feeling confused about which of my skills were perceived as lacking. I knew that I could be better at reference but never did I think I did not know how to conduct a reference interview.

I am so thankful that my coordinator did not believe the person who gave the report. Luckily for me, she had firsthand knowledge of my reference interview skills as we shared a reference desk shift. In addition to disputing the claim, she assured the person that she was quite pleased with my performance at the reference desk as she had witnessed my interactions with library users. She knew exactly what my strengths and weaknesses were, and reference was not one of the latter. How about that? In a profession where it has often been assumed that a problem might have occurred, it was a relief to know that the structure of the program allowed for some protection.

Mentorship is the gift that keeps on giving. Not only do I have the same mentor, I use every opportunity to form relationships with new(er) librarians and students. It is not enough to make way for one's success in the profession, but we must prepare the next generation of librarians. Do not be short-sighted to believe that mentors have to come from the library. Too, mentorship does not have to be a formal process. Instead, full integration into the organization will help the resident have a sense of belonging and give them confidence.

Organizational Support

Although this is my last recommendation on the success of resident programs, it could certainly be first on the list. Without a commitment from administration, the program will not be successful and residents may feel marginalized and microaggressed. As I have written, my experiences as a resident were overwhelmingly positive; however, there were times when I knew I was not respected as faculty. For a while, I had to constantly remind my colleagues that I was not an intern—as they commonly referred to me—as I had earned my degree, the same credential that they held. Although it was tiresome, I corrected them every time they misrepresented my title. I wanted to make sure that everyone knew I had every right to occupy that space. It was not fair to me, or any incoming resident, to have to contend with passive-aggressive attitudes that assumed UL could have hired a real librarian. As I remember, with the exclusion of Resident Program, UL had a slowed hiring of faculty, which left vacant positions some felt needed to be filled. So, when I was hired, it seemed as if there was a bit of tension about what role I would serve. It was a bit territorial and some egos were out of control as they did not see why the library had wasted a faculty line on a librarian fresh out of library school.

Most people were gracious, but I could sense that I would have to prove my worth to the organization. Part of me wonders if some were disappointed that they would not be able to pass their work off on me. You know, it is not all rosy and bright in library world. There is not a shortage of librarians who are looking for ways in which to make their workload lighter. In these cases, residents are like fresh meat on the savannah. A strong coordinator is absolutely essential if one is to have a resident program. The person should consider this as their vocation. Yep, I said it! Coordinators should have a desire to promote and facilitate the growth of residents. Librarians who are tenure-track should not accept a role as coordinator unless it is their primary function (tenure-track).

Outside of my duties at UL, I also had external opportunities for professional development. I was part of the inaugural class of ALA Emerging Leaders, and I attended national conferences. From these experiences, I enlarged my network of librarians and administrators. Additionally, I participated in regional professional development workshops with my colleagues. Even though the workshops were outside of my public services "home," I really enjoyed learning about technical services and other departments. One of my fondest memories was a training session at UNM Taos. My colleague and I took the university's old but trusty Chevy on the road (work can be fun) to a branch campus in the northern part of the state. Besides learning about how different the landscape of northern New Mexico is from Albuquerque, I also learned about the process to reserve university vehicles, the opportunities for larger libraries to help smaller libraries via resource sharing (human), and the importance of continual training. Monies for these activities have to be a part of the funding of the program. If administrators are resistant to provide funding for professional development, it is probably safe to assume they are not committed to the program and will find your requests (for such items) as borderline harassment.

Conclusion

The recommendations I have offered are but a few that coordinators should consider. Resident programs vary greatly and have the potential to provide a great introduction to academic librarianship. The resident program I participated in is no longer running. It ended about two years after I left. Coordinators should be aware that with changing administrators, one cannot guarantee that such initiatives will be valued/preserved. Lastly, whatever you do, resident programs should not be sole providers of racial diversity. If your program is charged with hiring librarians from racial minoritized groups, please be mindful that your organization could use this as a form of tokenism. A diversity resident program should not be their only avenue of hiring librarians of color, and they should evaluate whether or not they are retaining any of these residents as permanent hires. If not, what is this all for? Why are we hiring these librarians with no intention of keeping them? This should be a top priority for all coordinators for resident programs. Recruit. Hire. Retain!

⊚ Key Points

- Familiarizing staff with the purpose and goals of the residency before the resident comes to the institution is vital to ensuring success for both the institution and resident. In particular, those who will work closely with the resident should have ample time to prepare for his or her arrival.
- If possible, communicate with residents before they arrive to make sure they understand what areas they will begin working in, as well as information about when they will receive their first paycheck and when they begin accruing benefits. If possible, provide support to relocating residents to help them find housing.
- Undergo anti-bias and/or diversity training; provide opportunities for such training across the library organization.
- Create a residency handbook and other onboarding materials that explain the resident's role in the organization, as well as the roles of those with whom they will interact regularly, like the residency coordinator and area supervisors.

⊚ Notes

1. Jolie O. Graybill et al., "Employee Onboarding: Identification of Best Practices in ACRL Libraries," *Library Management* 34, no. 3 (2013): 200–218, doi:10.1108/01435121311310897; Lori Snyder and Erin Crane, "Developing and Implementing an Onboarding Program for an Academic Library: Strategies and Methods," *Library Leadership & Management* 30, no. 3 (2016); Angela Ballard and Laura Blessing, "Organizational Socialization through Employee Orientations at North Carolina State University Libraries," *College & Research Libraries* 67, no. 3 (2006): 240–48.

2. Bruce Keisling and Melissa Laning, "We Are Happy to Be Here: The Onboarding Experience in Academic Libraries," *Journal of Library Administration* 56, no. 4 (2016): 381–94.

3. Bonnie R. Strickland, "Acculturation," *The Gale Encyclopedia of Psychology* (Farmington Hills, Mich.: Gale, 2001).

4. Jean Barbazette, *Successful New Employee Orientation: A Step-by-Step Guide for Designing, Facilitating, and Evaluating Your Program* (San Francisco: Pfeiffer, 2007).

5. Jason Alston, "Causes of Satisfaction and Dissatisfaction for Diversity Resident Librarians—A Mixed Methods Study Using Herzberg's Motivation-Hygiene Theory" (Doctoral dissertation, University of South Carolina, 2017), scholarcommons.sc.edu/etd/4080; Chanelle Pickens and Ashleigh D. Coren, "Diversity Residency Programs: Strategies for a Collaborative Approach to Development," *Collaborative Librarianship* 9, no. 2 (2017): 6; Michael Fontenot, "Diversity: A Task Force: Survey of the Literature and Some Possible Trends for Academic Libraries," *Louisiana Libraries* 73, no. 1 (2010): 8–11; Sylvia S. Hu and Demetria E. Patrick, "Our Experience as Minority Residents: Benefits, Drawbacks, and Suggestions," *College & Research Libraries News* 67, no. 5 (2006): 297–300.

6. Julie Brewer and Mark D. Winston, "Program Evaluation for Internship/Residency Programs in Academic and Research Libraries," *College & Research Libraries* 62, no. 4 (2001): 307–15, doi:10.5860/crl.62.4.307.

7. Howard J. Klein, Beth Polin, and Kyra Leigh Sutton, "Specific Onboarding Practices for the Socialization of New Employees," *International Journal of Selection and Assessment* 23, no. 3 (2015): 263–83.

8. Graybill et al., "Employee Onboarding."

9. Kaetrena D. Kendrick, "Hold Up: The Impact of Diversity Rhetoric and Initiatives on Minority Academic Librarians" (Oral presentation, Metrolina Library Association Conference, Charlotte, N.C., 2018), prezi.com/opjo8to2k7xh/hold-up/.

10. Kaetrena Davis Kendrick, "The Low Morale Experience of Academic Librarians: A Phenomenological Study," *Journal of Library Administration* 57, no. 8 (November 17, 2017): 846–78, doi:10.1080/01930826.2017.1368325.

11. Julie Brewer, "Post-Master's Residency Programs: Enhancing the Development of New Professionals and Minority Recruitment in Academic and Research Libraries," *College & Research Libraries* 59, no. 6 (1998): 10.

12. "Diversity Counts" (American Library Association, 2012), www.ala.org/aboutala/sites/ala.org.aboutala/files/content/diversity/diversitycounts/diversitycountstables2012.pdf.

13. Angela Boyd, Yolanda Blue, and Suzanne Im, "Evaluation of Academic Library Residency Programs in the United States for Librarians of Color," *College & Research Libraries* 78, no. 4 (May 4, 2017): 472, doi:10.5860/crl.78.4.472; Linda DeBeau-Melting and Karen Beavers, "Positioning for Change: The Diversity Internship as a Good Beginning," in *Diversity and Multiculturalism in Libraries*, ed. Katherine Hoover Hill (Greenwich, Conn.: JAI Press, 1994); Kristin Heidi Gerhard and Jeanne M. K. Boydston, "A Library Committee on Diversity and Its Role in a Library Diversity Program," *College & Research Libraries* 54, no. 4 (July 1993): 9.

14. Keith Curry Lance, "Racial and Ethnic Diversity of U.S. Library Workers," *American Libraries*, May 2005.

15. Chester M. Pierce et al., "An Experiment in Racism: TV Commercials," *Education and Urban Society* 10, no. 1 (1977): 61–87.

16. Rosalinda Hernandez Linares and Sojourna J. Cunningham, "Small Brown Faces in Large White Spaces," in *Pushing the Margins: Women of Color and Intersectionality in LIS*, Series on Critical Race Studies and Multiculturalism in LIS 3 (Sacramento, Cal.: Library Juice Press, 2018), 253–72.

17. Fobazi Ettarh, "Vocational Awe and Librarianship: The Lies We Tell Ourselves," *In the Library with the Lead Pipe*, January 10, 2018, www.inthelibrarywiththeleadpipe.org/2018/vocational-awe/.

18. Eleanor A. LaPointe, "Tokenism," *Salem Press Encyclopedia*, 2014, proxy.library.stonybrook.edu/login?url=http://search.ebscohost.com/login.aspx?direct=true&db=ers&AN=96397717&site=eds-live&scope=site; Raquel V. Cogell and Cindy A. Gruwell, eds., *Diversity in Libraries: Academic Residency Programs* (Westport, Conn.: Greenwood Press, 2001).

19. Chanelle Pickens and Ashleigh D. Coren. "Diversity Residency Programs: Strategies for a Collaborative Approach to Development." *Collaborative Librarianship* 9, no. 2 (2017): 7.

References

Alston, Jason. "Causes of Satisfaction and Dissatisfaction for Diversity Resident Librarians—A Mixed Methods Study Using Herzberg's Motivation-Hygiene Theory." Doctoral dissertation, University of South Carolina, 2017. scholarcommons.sc.edu/etd/4080.

Ballard, Angela, and Laura Blessing. "Organizational Socialization through Employee Orientations at North Carolina State University Libraries." *College & Research Libraries* 67, no. 3 (2006): 240–48.

Barbazette, Jean. *Successful New Employee Orientation: A Step-by-Step Guide for Designing, Facilitating, and Evaluating Your Program.* San Francisco: Pfeiffer, 2007.

Boyd, Angela, Yolanda Blue, and Suzanne Im. "Evaluation of Academic Library Residency Programs in the United States for Librarians of Color." *College & Research Libraries* 78, no. 4 (May 4, 2017): 472. doi:10.5860/crl.78.4.472.

Brewer, Julie. "Post-Master's Residency Programs: Enhancing the Development of New Professionals and Minority Recruitment in Academic and Research Libraries." *College & Research Libraries* 59, no. 6 (1998): 10.

Brewer, Julie, and Mark D. Winston. "Program Evaluation for Internship/Residency Programs in Academic and Research Libraries." *College & Research Libraries* 62, no. 4 (2001): 307–15. doi:10.5860/crl.62.4.307.

Cogell, Raquel V., and Cindy A. Gruwell, eds. *Diversity in Libraries: Academic Residency Programs.* Westport, Conn.: Greenwood Press, 2001.

DeBeau-Melting, Linda, and Karen Beavers. "Positioning for Change: The Diversity Internship as a Good Beginning." In *Diversity and Multiculturalism in Libraries*, ed. Katherine Hoover Hill. Greenwich, Conn.: JAI Press, 1994.

"Diversity Counts." American Library Association, 2012. www.ala.org/aboutala/sites/ala.org .aboutala/files/content/diversity/diversitycounts/diversitycountstables2012.pdf.

Ettarh, Fobazi. "Vocational Awe and Librarianship: The Lies We Tell Ourselves." *In the Library with the Lead Pipe*, January 10, 2018. www.inthelibrarywiththeleadpipe.org/2018/vocational -awe/.

Fontenot, Michael. "Diversity: A Task Force: Survey of the Literature and Some Possible Trends for Academic Libraries." *Louisiana Libraries* 73, no. 1 (2010): 8–11.

Gerhard, Kristin Heidi, and Jeanne M. K. Boydston. "A Library Committee on Diversity and Its Role in a Library Diversity Program." *College & Research Libraries* 54, no. 4 (July 1993): 9.

Graybill, Jolie O., Maria Taesil Hudson Carpenter, Jerome Offord, Mary Piorun, and Gary Shaffer. "Employee Onboarding: Identification of Best Practices in ACRL Libraries." *Library Management* 34, no. 3 (2013): 200–218. doi:https://doi.org/10.1108/01435121311310897.

Hernandez Linares, Rosalinda, and Sojourna Cunningham J. "Small Brown Faces in Large White Spaces." In *Pushing the Margins: Women of Color and Intersectionality in LIS*, 253–72. Series on Critical Race Studies and Multiculturalism in LIS 3. Sacramento, Cal.: Library Juice Press, 2018.

Hu, Sylvia S., and Demetria E. Patrick. "Our Experience as Minority Residents: Benefits, Drawbacks, and Suggestions." *College & Research Libraries News* 67, no. 5 (2006): 297–300.

Keisling, Bruce, and Melissa Laning. "We Are Happy to Be Here: The Onboarding Experience in Academic Libraries." *Journal of Library Administration* 56, no. 4 (2016): 381–94.

Kendrick, Kaetrena D. "Hold Up: The Impact of Diversity Rhetoric and Initiatives on Minority Academic Librarians." Oral presentation presented at the Metrolina Library Association Conference, Charlotte, N.C., 2018. prezi.com/opjo8to2k7xh/hold-up/.

———. "The Low Morale Experience of Academic Librarians: A Phenomenological Study." *Journal of Library Administration* 57, no. 8 (November 17, 2017): 846–78. doi:10.1080/0193 0826.2017.1368325.

Klein, Howard J., Beth Polin, and Kyra Leigh Sutton. "Specific Onboarding Practices for the Socialization of New Employees." *International Journal of Selection and Assessment* 23, no. 3 (2015): 263–83.

Lance, Keith Curry. "Racial and Ethnic Diversity of U.S. Library Workers." *American Libraries*, May 2005.

LaPointe, Eleanor A. "Tokenism." *Salem Press Encyclopedia*, 2014. proxy.library.stonybrook.edu/ login?url=http://search.ebscohost.com/login.aspx?direct=true&db=ers&AN=96397717& site=eds-live&scope=site.

Pickens, Chanelle, and Ashleigh D. Coren. "Diversity Residency Programs: Strategies for a Collaborative Approach to Development." *Collaborative Librarianship* 9, no. 2 (2017): 6.

Pierce, Chester M., Jean V. Carew, Diane Pierce-Gonzalez, and Deborah Wills. "An Experiment in Racism: TV Commercials." *Education and Urban Society* 10, no. 1 (1977): 61–87.

Snyder, Lori, and Erin Crane. "Developing and Implementing an Onboarding Program for an Academic Library: Strategies and Methods." *Library Leadership & Management* 30, no. 3 (2016).

Strickland, Bonnie R. "Acculturation." *The Gale Encyclopedia of Psychology.* Farmington Hills, Mich.: Gale, 2001.

Onboarding

Resident's Arrival and Beyond

A FIRST RESIDENT'S ARRIVAL, and any new resident's arrival, for that matter, is an exciting time during which much of the preparation work by coordinators, administrators, work supervisors, and mentors involved in the residency program comes to fruition. It is a point at which the residency program transitions from being a conceptual framework to a living operation in the library, embodied by a real resident. Building on the intentional preparations detailed in the previous chapters, this chapter describes best practices for onboarding once the resident has actually arrived.

Setting Up and Coordinating Orientations

Many of the actions listed on the onboarding checklists that you built prior to the resident's arrival likely involve orientations (see table 7.1). In many institutions, human resources departments may already require all new employees to attend at least one institutional orientation session shortly after their start date at the institution. Particularly in large academic libraries, there may already be an existing combination of institutional orientation and library orientation(s) in place. The institutional orientation usually covers broad topics such as benefits information, workplace conduct and safety policies, information about major institutional partnerships with community organizations, and so on. Be aware that while these orientations are important, in part because they provide an opportunity to fulfill important transactional tasks such as paperwork, they are not by themselves sufficient as a means of socializing new personnel to an organization's mission, values, and culture.[1]

Depending on the type of residency, a resident may undergo several types of orientations, including a human resources orientation, a library orientation, and at least one department or work area orientation. If the resident will work in more than one department or area, they may receive more than one of the latter type. Given the strategic component of many residency programs, and the expectation in many residency programs that the resident will grow familiar with and work with many figures across the library or institution, it makes sense to provide a broad program of orientations. However, it's also important to provide enough time for the resident to digest and learn the new information.

Graybill et al.[2] accumulate a substantial list of topics to be covered in orientations through their literature review, many of which fit well into library and/or department orientations for residents. These include:

- review of policies;
- review of safety procedures;
- explanation of position (at the department level, this may be a discussion of work to be performed);
- introduction to structures and workflows and where the resident is located within these;
- introductions to colleagues;
- tours; and
- explanation of communication channels.

If the resident is expected to undergo orientations at not only the institution and library levels but also the department or work area level shortly after their start date, it may be advisable to consider the spacing of the orientations, to ensure that the three orientations do not overwhelm the new resident. To this end, including the resident's department or work supervisors (as mentioned in chapter 7) can help to ensure that the multiple orientations are given in bite-sized pieces and that they do not unduly duplicate coverage. Coordinating orientations can help to mitigate some forms of new job stress for the resident.

⊚ Understanding and Ameliorating New Job Stress

It is more or less inevitable that a new employee will experience uncertainty or stress in a new environment. New residents may experience this in particular ways; the residency may be one of their first jobs in the library profession and/or in your library type. For some, it may be a first full-time job or a job for which they relocated to a place in which they have no connections. Substantial literature points out that designing an onboarding process to allay new job stress can also help to maximize the employee's capacity and desire to adjust to the organization and learn job functions.[3]

Seeing "onboarding" as a process that works to allay a new employee's stress can illuminate ways in which you can meaningfully support your resident. While this view complements a more common view of onboarding as a process that maximizes a new employee's performance, it also emphasizes the resident's experience of the onboarding process, with less of an implicit expectation that they owe the organization a performance of high function and happiness due to the organization's investment. Commonly cited potential stressors for new employees include:[4]

- unclear job scope or role ambiguity,
- pressure to acquire new skills for job functions,
- pressure to acquire new cultural behaviors for the workplace,
- lack of existing social circles in the workplace,
- recent relocation,
- financial stresses,
- time pressures,
- workload, and
- uncertainty about advancement opportunities.

Several of these can hold particular weight for residents, especially role ambiguity, financial stresses, and time pressure. For considerations and ideas for supporting residents around financial stresses, please see chapter 7.

Role Ambiguity

Edmonson defines role ambiguity as something that happens when "people are unclear or uncertain about their expectations within a certain role,"[5] often due to a lack of specificity in the way the person's job is defined. Many residents experience some stress from uncertain job scopes and ambiguity in their roles; this may sometimes manifest as impostor syndrome.[6] Many factors can contribute to role ambiguity; for example, Oates cites the true-entry-level nature of residency positions, as well as general confusion between residencies and internships, as a factor in colleagues' views of her capabilities as a resident (see chapter 7). Other factors include the term limitation of residencies, the roving nature of rotational residencies, and tokenism in diversity residencies.[7]

Imagine the following scenarios:

- Shereen is a resident working in the reference department; she asks for projects to work on during time not spent on the reference desk and is given small office tasks to perform. Sometime thereafter, Shereen's colleagues express some surprise that Shereen has completed library school and note, "You should have said something."
- Enwar is rotating in a busy library department and asks several colleagues if he can contribute to their collaborative projects. Each colleague expresses that they wish they could include Enwar, but they aren't sure if they can include a contributor who will leave the department in a few months.
- Lea is speaking with some teaching faculty at an event to drum up interest in a library exhibit that she created. The teaching faculty members express interest and ask what Lea's position at the library is. Lea indicates that she is a resident librarian; the faculty members ask her to clarify, which requires two or three exchanges. After this, the conversation moves to other topics, and Lea's exhibit is forgotten.

In each of these scenarios, role ambiguity impedes the progression of meaningful collaboration and work experiences for the resident. Be aware of the factors that can lead to role ambiguity regarding a library residency position, and be ready to reinforce an expectation among the resident's colleagues that the resident is, first and foremost, a qualified professional who may learn on the job but can nevertheless contribute significantly while doing so. It may be helpful to preemptively address common misconceptions prior to the resident's arrival (see chapter 7). These misconceptions include ideas that residents are less valuable due to the term-limited nature of their position or that a rotational resident cannot make significant contributions in the limited time frame of a rotation. Not only does addressing these misconceptions help to set some expectations before the resident's arrival, but having this language on-hand when the resident does arrive may help them self-advocate when they inevitably encounters confusion or hesitation related to their roles and position.

In diversity residencies that aim to attract candidates of underrepresented backgrounds, it may be particularly significant to remind the resident's colleagues before the resident arrives that there is a distinction between the purpose of the residency program and the goals of the individual resident. Role ambiguity for a diversity residency may be complicated by tacit misconceptions that the resident's primary role is bodily representation of diversity because the program's mission includes building capacity to hire and retain diverse professionals. It's important to note that the program may include increasing diversity of the organization or the profession among its goals in some way, but the resident has their own individual purposes and goals. The program meets its goal of increasing the organization's capacity to hire and retain diverse librarians by helping the resident meet their individual purposes and goals. While this may seem like common sense, it does not always go without saying that the resident is not there to simply embody Otherness and that to imply this or allow the resident to be treated as such, even in indirect ways, is degrading and belittles his or her capabilities and potential as a librarian.

As is likely clear, the issue of role ambiguity in the resident's job description is rarely the only stressor that a resident may face. It often interacts with other stressors, such as time pressures related to the length of a rotation and stress regarding future job prospects after the residency. Allaying this particular stressor can play an important role in ensuring that the resident has sufficient capacity to handle other stressors.

In a study focusing on new-employee onboarding in the hospitality industry, Yang[8] finds that role ambiguity and role conflict negatively affect the acquisition of job competencies and that enabling social interaction is positively correlated with building job competencies. While it does not necessarily follow that enabling and supporting a resident's social interactions with colleagues directly counteracts the effects of role ambiguity, it is possible that doing so allows the resident to meet individuals who may become key to their work later on. Furthermore, for many staff members who don't yet play direct roles in the residency program, meeting and building relationships with a resident in person may be the main means by which the residency position becomes understandable as having specific roles, which may lead to further buy-in.

Caldwell and Caldwell[9] place much of the responsibility for anticipating and ameliorating role ambiguity on management. They frame new-employee socialization in terms of the formation of a psychological contract, or a belief in a set of explicit and implicit mutual obligations between employers and employees; many of the "classic onboarding errors" that they name are framed as breaches of the psychological contract. These include:

failure to communicate the full range of job expectations in a realistic and timely fashion, delay or failure in providing routine vital information, and neglecting to support the new employee's ability to build relationships with individuals and networks key to the success of their work. Consider how to avoid these errors or counteract their effects throughout the resident's orientation and onboarding by:

- scheduling a specific time during orientation to go over job expectations;
- scheduling specific times during milestone check-ins to ensure that expectations on both sides remain the same or that new expectations are mutually agreed upon;
- providing the resident with a handbook of vital information (see chapter 7) and adding to it as necessary; and
- enabling and facilitating introductions to individuals and networks performing roles that are related to the resident's interests or key to the resident's upcoming work.

Time Pressures

As occupants of a position term-limited to one to three years, residents have a reduced time frame in which to learn about the library's culture and acclimate to it than most permanent and permanent-track staff do. Common literature estimates that workplace socialization and acclimation to workplace culture may take at least a year.[10] As stated in chapter 6, this can mean that the resident spends a large portion of their residency learning to navigate and negotiate in the workplace. To add to this, many residencies split the residency up into an exploratory or learning period, in which the resident explores interests or rotates through multiple areas, and a project period in which the resident leads or performs a significant long-term project (usually at least a year). Particularly in rotational residencies, while the resident is in the exploratory period, they may only have short time frames of a few months in which to perform projects that their work supervisors may assign them. Last but not least, the last six to twelve months of the residency are often particularly pressured by the resident's search for a new job after the residency, in some cases, at the same time as their significant long-term project.

With these factors in mind, you can help your resident navigate some of these time pressures in a few ways:

- Check in with the resident regularly as their work progresses to ensure that the work they are performing is both meaningful as work experience and also a reasonable amount of work for them to do in the given time period.
- Ensure that the resident, the coordinator, and the work supervisor(s) are all on the same page regarding the resident's time commitments, including not only his work projects but also committee service, upcoming conference attendance, and other commitments.
- Review the time needs of early projects; use this information to iteratively review and inform expectations of time commitments as the resident takes on new projects.

As briefly noted in chapter 7, this last point can make it possible to perform iterative planning for the program's structure and guidelines and to assess the program's success.

If you use the resident work log method, remember to take into account how your request that the resident log their work may impact the resident. There may be tacit messaging in being asked to track one's time and work completion timelines, particularly if no other employee does so as formally. For example, this may effectively tell the resident that they are under higher scrutiny or surveillance than other librarians due to their early-career status. Take care to address why you are asking the resident to log their work, and take care not to use the work log for purposes beyond what you tell the resident it is to be used for.

⊚ Setting Up Regular Support Mechanisms

As stated above, orientations play an important role in onboarding; however, it is not generally realistic to expect that one-shot orientations will cover the entirety of what new residents need to know in order to perform their jobs and acclimate to a new organization, a new position, and new colleagues. Thus, residency coordinators, administrators, supervisors of residents, and other individuals with roles in the residency program should also consider aspects of onboarding that need to be covered after orientations, as the resident begins their work.

The milestone check-ins mentioned in chapter 7 (thirty days, three months, six months, twelve months) can help to form a basic rapport with residents to ensure that you understand their needs. You may choose to check in more frequently with the resident to strengthen that rapport; this can ensure timely support of immediate needs, help build the resident's awareness of what types of support to expect from whom, and provide a regular forum in which to discuss issues that may crop up slowly, over the course of several months. This can serve to build the resident's expectation that they have opportunities to express patterns that they perceive over time in their residency experience. You may also find that the resident becomes more open regarding their professional interests and goals and how they would like the program to enable them to pursue these, as your conversation becomes more regular. If the resident has been led to expect check-ins at a specific frequency, avoid changing that frequency without their input. If regular check-ins on programmatic issues have been built into a role occupied by someone other than the residency coordinator, such as a residency mentor, ensure that that person is empowered to respond to the resident's requests and organize arrangements or accommodations according to immediate needs that may surface in the check-ins. Be aware that these check-ins may surface many types of needs requiring administrative support, such as travel and professional development, adjusting plans for upcoming rotations, and requesting reasonable workplace accommodations for a short- or long-term disability.

Check-ins, regardless of their frequency, present a strong opportunity to build a dialogue with the resident about their interests and their experience of the program. They help to ensure that the resident's goals and interests are accurately reflected in the program's assessment goals; if the resident's goals and interests evolve based on their experience, it is important to respond to this and ensure that this change is reflected in your assessment of the program. Check-ins can provide a way for you to find out if residents are learning what they wanted or needed to learn and if they are empowered to contribute in areas that they aim to make impacts in. They may also be used to ensure that there are multiple opportunities to reflect on past, current, and upcoming events and experiences within the program. Iterative reflection can surface many observations over time, and allowing the resident opportunities to reflect iteratively can enrich informal and formal program assessment in a way that simple before-and-after interviews may not.

Mentorship

Mentorship is a significant way to support early-career professionals and can be built into and supported in the program in multiple ways. Many residency programs include an assigned mentor for the resident. Mentor roles differ by program but by and large are generally intended to provide the resident with an experienced advisor on the library's services and culture and on librarianship as a profession. Mentors can also play a role of introducing residents who relocated to the institution's locale or helping the residents plan their professional development. In academic libraries, mentors may also serve to introduce the residents to the campus community, including bringing them to meetings and events.

Even in programs with assigned mentors, the residents may naturally form organic or informal advisory relationships with individuals who may not be their assigned mentor. Generally, this is an indicator that the residents are forming connections that fit their needs within the institution and should be encouraged;[11] the more experienced and trusted advisors an early-career professional has, the better.

Mentorship may also come from professional development programs and networking outside of your institution. Generally, attending conferences and engaging in other professional service and learning opportunities can enable the residents to build a network to support their professional growth, not only during their residency but throughout their careers. For this reason, it is important to provide financial support for the residents' professional development. Joanna Chen Cham highlights multiple examples of this in her own residency experience, contributed to chapter 4. Many library associations have mentorship programs that may allow a resident to find a mentor within a particular community of library practitioners. Additionally, providing the resident with substantial financial support for professional development can enable residents to find communities of peer practitioners. Peer mentors can form an important dimension of the resident's support network, not least because peer mentoring relationships involve a mutuality that cannot be matched in traditional mentoring relationships predicated on the mentor possessing and imparting professional knowledge that the mentee does not have. Hannah Lee Park's residency experience, highlighted in chapter 10, brings forth the ways in which formal mentoring and peer mentoring are valuable to residents. Park states that she was particularly proactive in seeking ways to fill gaps in her program; providing means for residents to seek mentoring relationships throughout the profession is thus an important means of enabling residents to fulfill some of their own needs.

Providing Support for Research and Professional Development

One of the main purposes of a residency program is to provide the resident or residents with concentrated professional development and mentorship. Early in a librarian's career, it is important for the resident to carve out a space for themselves in the professional community. Especially in academic librarianship, librarians are expected to have a research agenda and scholarly output to advance in their careers. If residents begin this process sooner rather than later, they will have a strong foundation on which to build their academic and professional career.

Some residents might already have an idea of what they would like to research and where to present that research. Others, however, might not. As a residency coordinator, you can offer advice to your residents as to how they should get started. If the resident has other mentors, hearing other perspectives is helpful as well.

Developing a Research Agenda

A question you or your resident might have is, what is a research agenda? According to *Inside Higher Ed*, a research agenda is a "plan and a focus on issues and ideas in a subset of your field."[12] This definition stresses the importance that you cannot and should not study or master every possible subset of librarianship; it is far more important to specialize in one area. A research agenda also does not have to be set in stone. As each resident progresses in their specialty, their research agenda can and should change with them. They might also change their agenda entirely!

To help your resident develop their own research agenda, a first step might be to have a conversation with your resident about what interests them. Were there articles they read in grad school they enjoyed? Have they heard of an area and wants to explore it? Is there a scholar they respect? Is there a problem in librarianship that they feel driven to investigate and possibly fix? Perhaps you could create a shared document where you can both edit the document and share ideas and comments! A next step might be to share your research agenda with the resident and how you decided on it. Then, have them talk with other faculty members and colleagues outside of your institution.

Is your resident on social media? Consider encouraging them to network on Twitter! Many librarians have personal Twitter accounts and are more than happy to meet new people. If the subjective line of "professional versus personal" comes into question, you can let your resident know that many librarians keep a professional account and a personal account for separate use.

Now that your resident has an idea as to what research areas are of interest to them, you can help them to navigate the scholarly literature relating to that area. When they identify key authors in that area, have your resident contact that author or make the connection yourself. By speaking with authors and becoming familiar with the subject area, your resident can plan what work they will need to do in their area and how to best have that scholarly conversation. And when they are ready to go to the next step and be a part of that conversation, you can help them decide where to present and publish.

Choosing and Attending Conferences

Conferences can be overwhelming: traveling, presenting, meeting new people, networking, self-care. It all adds up. But attending conferences is a crucial aspect of professional development and scholarly communication in the library profession. Probably, your resident has at least heard of the major national organizations like the American Library Association (ALA). In fact, they may have even been involved with a student chapter or are already members of these organizations. Attending the ALA Midwinter and Annual conferences allows librarians to network with colleagues all over the world as well as to expand their knowledge in their discipline. However, keep in mind that both ALA conferences are very large and busy. As such, going to one of these as a first conference may not be the right path, since large conferences can be cost-prohibitive and incredibly socially overwhelming.

Instead of throwing your resident into the deep end, go over alternative conference options. State library association conferences are an excellent place to not only start becoming involved in professional service but also to ease into conference attendance. Specialized organizations, such as the Digital Library Federation and the Online Audiovisual Catalogers, also offer conferences and are usually much smaller and less expensive. If your resident is interested in subject librarianship, you can also encourage them to attend conferences outside of librarianship in his interest subject.[13] Another avenue is to attend conferences that your patron base might go to. For instance, in Utah, genealogical research is popular, so some librarians will attend conferences in that area in order to understand where patrons are coming from.

If cost is an issue, many conferences offer travel scholarships as well as volunteer opportunities to help reduce or waive the cost of attendance; your program should also give your resident adequate travel money to accommodate the need for professional development.

If your resident wants to go a step further and present at a conference, poster presentations are an excellent first step. Most poster submissions only require an abstract or maybe a small paper instead of a full-length article submission. Posters are also a good way for your resident to get used to presenting at the regional or national level. Another option is to work on a project with your resident and submit proposals for workshops or presentations together!

Getting the Most Out of Conferences

You can encourage your residents to participate in conferences but that does not mean that they will know what to do once they are there. Instead, you should also give your residents a primer on what to expect from conferences and how to get the most benefit from attending.

Your residents might want to know why they should attend conferences outside of the professional development reasons. In the article "Top Six Reasons to Attend a Conference," Rosina Alaimo mentions other powerful reasons, such as the keynote speaker and the exhibits hall.[14] Another article mentions how important it is to keep up with current and developing trends within the profession, considering our profession interacts with technology so frequently.[15] Also, conferences can be really fun! Outside of the conference activities, there are always plenty of meetups and receptions where people can meet.

To help your residents get the most out of conferences, make sure you are familiar with the culture of the organization or conference. That way, you can let your residents know a few things: how big it is, how casual or professional it is, how practical or theoretical it is, what type of sessions are most common. Also make sure to bring up the more practical parts of attending conferences, like making sure your resident has comfortable but professional clothing, good walking shoes, a water bottle, and a way to take notes.

Publishing

Although your residents may not get to this point during their residency, you should be prepared to offer advice when considering pursuing publication. There are hundreds of possible venues to publish one's research, and it can be difficult to decide which journal would be a good fit for their research and writing style. As a benefit to your residents as

A couple of best practices to consider:

1. Write an abstract and send it to the editor(s) of the journal you want to publish in. Ask if there is interest for a full article.
2. Read through articles recently published for the journal you want to publish in. What style is used? How are the abstracts worded? Use a similar style in your writing.

Excellent lib guide from USC on key Library and Information Science Journals

Advances in Library Administration and Organization (Book Series)

This book series was initiated to publish longer, quality research studies, of interest both to working library managers and scholars. We are particularly interested in how libraries have been and should be managed.

Behavioral & Social Sciences Librarian

College and Research Libraries

Digital Humanities Quarterly

An open-access, peer-reviewed, digital journal covering all aspects of digital media in the humanities. Published by the Alliance of Digital Humanities Organizations (ADHO). Digital humanities is a diverse and still emerging field that encompasses the practice of humanities research in and through information technology, and the exploration of how the humanities may evolve through their engagement with

Figure 8.1. Screenshot of possible publication venues for library faculty at the University of Utah

well as the rest of your colleagues, you might encourage your library to curate a list of possible publishing venues with links to guidelines for authors.

You can review these guidelines with your residents and study the scopes of the journals. And if your residents submit an article and it is rejected, assure them that it does not mean that their article is bad but merely that it might not be a good fit for that journal.

Considerations and Potential Pitfalls

Building Inclusion and Support in Onboarding for Diversity Residencies

Residency coordinators and administrators should critically examine onboarding processes to consider where they present barriers to the retention of diverse talent and work to mitigate them. The onboarding planning and process should include consistent internal questioning of whether your internal expectations, such as what successful "socialization to the organizational culture" looks like or what constitutes "professional behavior," match the espoused desires to diversify. There is a general tendency to evaluate new employees following their onboarding partially based on how well they have adapted to organizational culture. While this evaluative framing is understandable, it tends to perpetuate the cultural status quo, creating a hostile environment for many people with marginalized identities who are surrounded by a culture that does not account for their lived experience. It is important to critically consider whether the library's ability to retain culturally diverse employees is related to how open the organization is to expanding what its organizational culture has room for. The concepts of "cultural fit" and "professionalism" are often misused to mask internal bias in personnel processes like evaluation.[16] In training new residents, trainers should try to be open to residents' approaches to professionalism and workplace acculturation and avoid prescribing behavioral changes, such as hairstyle changes or conversational tone changes, without full awareness of their cultural significance and how changing them may impact the resident's ability to grow and thrive in the workplace. Just as in the interview process, trainers should also acknowledge and draw on the value of the resident's work experience in related sectors (such as customer service) as much as they would work experience in a similar library.

If your organization seeks to evaluate and shift its general strategy for diverse recruitment and retention, then by no means should these considerations be limited only to recruiting, hiring, and onboarding for the diversity residency. A residency can and should serve only as one initiative in an organization's plan to diversify; it may serve as the first site at which an organization seeks to consider the lived realities of professionals embodying marginalized identities but should certainly not be the last.

Furthermore, diversity is not achieved simply through recruiting and hiring, or the creation of what is often referred to as an LIS "pipeline."[17] Literature indicates that failing to build a culture of inclusion to support new staff of marginalized and oppressed identities creates a problem of attrition;[18] people of diverse minoritized identities leave the profession nearly as often as they are hired. This is because institutions, including libraries, that have not historically hired people of color, Native and Indigenous people, people with disabilities, people who observe minoritized religions, LGBTQIA* people, or other minoritized people do not usually have institutional cultures built to support an influx of people with marginalized and oppressed backgrounds. Diversity is only sustainable in the presence of a willingness by the entire organization to shift its culture to become more inclusive. Toward this end, it is suggested that residency program administrators and all individuals working closely with the residents should broadly discuss and thoroughly understand the mission and goals of the program, both as a residency program and as a diversity program, and undergo substantial diversity and inclusion training.[19]

Realistically, the work of building an inclusive workplace culture is a long-term project, rather than the product of single trainings.[20] However, it is important to at least begin engaging in this work prior to a resident's arrival and to take on the primary responsibility of interrogating the inclusiveness of your library's policies and culture during and after the term of any given resident, rather than expecting the resident to bear the extreme burden of both learning and changing organizational culture themselves.

Iterative Reflection Opportunities

Many residency programs already implement reflective opportunities for residents, rotation supervisors, mentors, coordinators, and other program participants in their assessment practices. It is recommended that reflection opportunities be provided on an iterative basis; that is to say, for example, rather than soliciting reflection on a first rotation and then closing the book on it, reflection should be encouraged iteratively throughout the residency. For some, an information gap from the onboarding process may not manifest until the residency term is more than halfway through. For others, the simple opportunity to adjust one's understanding of early experiences based on later experiences may prove helpful. Providing multiple opportunities for residents to contextualize experiences over time can be a significant way of supporting learning about and adjustment to the workplace. If shared with the coordinator or supervisor in evaluations or check-ins, iterative reflection can also provide a fuller picture of the resident's experience with which to assess the program.

Mitigating Labor Precarity

Library residencies are, by definition, temporary or contingent positions. Most residencies last between one and three years. This time frame is excellent for helping a resident build the necessary skills to enter into more permanent or even tenure-track positions, as even entry-level positions tend to require two years of experience. However, temporary positions can have negative impacts on both the resident and the institution if they are not considered beforehand.

Residents, even in the best circumstances, may feel a sense of labor precarity, or "existential, financial, and social insecurity exacerbated by the flexibilization of labor markets."[21] In addition to general new job stress, which is briefly covered above (see the "Understanding and Ameliorating New Job Stress" section), residents may have concerns about continuing employment or work-life balance. Many may fear that pursuing work-life balance or saying no to projects will make them seem like they are not go-getters, thus jeopardizing their opportunities for future employment. Labor precarity has been shown to correlate with poor mental health[22] and reduced investment in the workplace,[23] and it disproportionately affects workers from marginalized groups.[24] In this case, it is helpful for supervisors, mentors, and library administrators to recognize these challenges and support the resident in the following ways:

- helping the resident prioritize projects and avoid burnout,
- encouraging work/life balance, and
- providing the resident with ample resources in the search for continued employment.

Since residents may be in unequal power relationships with colleagues who want their help on various projects, supervisors in particular have an important role to play in helping the resident avoid becoming inundated with projects. Supervisors can also help protect the residents from being assigned projects with low priority or importance, ensuring that their time as residents is well-spent and that their work is their own and appropriate for further career expansion.

To prepare supervisors for the work of protecting and advocating for a resident's status and work-life balance, consider doing research on labor advocacy and best practices. If your resident is eligible to join a union, encourage them to do so, and if not, put your resident in contact with their human resources representative for workplace issues and concerns. If your resident is salaried, do your best to ensure that they are not regularly required to work on their personal or "off" time; although it is sometimes impossible to finish one's work in a work week, overtime work is not compensated in salaried positions. As delineated in the autoethnography below, it is also important to take the time to listen when your resident expresses needs, values, or boundaries. This creates a supportive atmosphere, which enables open and honest conversations regarding the workplace's culture and norms and how to navigate them while maintaining a healthy work-life balance.

Outside of work, temporary positions affect the personal lives of residents when making long-term decisions, such as when, how, or if to pursue platonic or romantic relationships. When only living in a place for a few years, settling into a community is a difficult task. The residency coordinator or others in the institution can help the resident explore opportunities for connecting and thriving in a community.[25] If your institution has a faculty club or something similar for their job designation, let them

As part of onboarding, ask your residents if they want suggestions for good restaurants, parks, theaters, or other opportunities for engaging in their community.

know and encourage them to go. If you are not aware of appropriate social opportunities, find them someone who is.

Temporary positions like residencies can create flexibility; with planning and strong mentorship, it is possible to mitigate negative impacts of labor precarity, while maximizing the residents' opportunity to explore different avenues in their careers before settling into something more permanent.[26]

ALL THAT GLITTERS IS NOT GOLD: CRITICAL PERSPECTIVES ON LIBRARIAN RESIDENCIES
by Anonymous

Nearing the end of my two-year residency term, I have much to share with regard to residency programs, but I can only speak to my personal and unique experiences. I know and acknowledge that not all residency programs are the same and that experiences will vary between people. Philosophies that shape residency programs also vary between institutions. To what I lived over the past twenty-three months, I can say that my feeling toward residencies has grown equally as critical as I had been optimistic of this unique opportunity.

My program began in 2016. The librarian job I had prior to my residency was confronted by low morale and even lower participation by the public in programming. Things felt bleak, and I knew I had to get out. It was complete luck that I was able to interview and land a two-year residency and move toward academic librarianship. The structure that I had been promised was three to four rotations in departments of my choosing, undertaking projects that would speak to the skill set I wanted to have when entering the job market after my program was over. I was assigned a supervisor, but I would have a secondary manager in each department. Each rotation would last roughly five months, and any leftover time of my residency would be used to work in one of the chosen departments more closely until the residency was over. An added incentive was institutional support to travel to conferences as well to share any work that I did at the university. What early-career librarian wouldn't take such an opportunity?

Nevertheless, in progressing through the first few months of the residency, several things became clear: the structure was not as well defined as I had thought, and the institution as a whole—that is, my colleagues—did not know how to prepare me for advancement in the profession. Yet still I remained optimistic. In my rotation with the reference department, I was given the opportunity to take on reference desk shifts and conduct instruction sessions, and I took on several assessment projects. I can say that these experiences did bolster my experience and made me a stronger candidate on paper; however, a leadership component and a deeper understanding of reference librarianship were lacking, and it made it challenging to speak confidently and in depth about this branch of librarianship in interviews.

Returning to my point about the institution not knowing how to aid my advancement, this first rotation was where it became clear. I did not meet with my rotation supervisor to talk about finding a job in reference after the residency was over. We did not speak about emerging trends and technologies or the direction of the field of reference librarianship. We did not speak about how competitive it would be either. This also happened in one of my later rotations. The projects that I was assigned were not ones that I particularly had interest in, but since they were presented to me by my rotation supervisor, and feeling naïve and not knowing what to expect of a residency, I felt they were my only options. I was given a list of projects to choose from, all of which seemed to be small responsibilities as part of bigger projects or that the department did not want to take on. I knew it would be hard to market myself for jobs in reference if I did not have the experience necessary where I was allowed to demonstrate leadership. While I appreciated the chance to do these projects, I knew that a very integral component of this experience was absent.

My rotation with the Digital Library was more enjoyable, given that the goals I had for myself in that department were heard. Unfortunately, there were conflicts in administration between these goals and the projects they wanted me undertake, and ultimately this rotation did not turn out to be all I had hoped it would be. I had wanted to gain digital storytelling skills using Omeka or Scalar, but it was decided for me that instead I should learn how digital materials are added to our institutional repository, so my rotation was ultimately altered. I appreciated the chance to become part of the department and learn how materials are digitized and how to use Dublin Core standards nonetheless.

I was able to accomplish the most in my rotation with Archives, and I learned to be more assertive and vocal about the projects I wanted to take on; however, problems arose with regard to ownership. For example, my first task in this rotation was to develop a guide to conduct oral histories. Once this guide was completed, I was reprimanded later for submitting a proposal to talk about it at a conference and for not mentioning in the proposal my rotation supervisor, even though I had been in charge of the majority of the work. This contributed to the feeling that I could not claim ownership of projects or demonstrate leadership in my residency.

A second example of this was when I was deciding with my rotation supervisor the projects I wanted to take on. I had proposed to bolster the University Archives material about a particular minority student group on campus, but I was ultimately told that "that was not a priority" for the department. Not only was this disappointing as a resident, or as a person of color working on a predominantly white campus, but also because it upheld the reality that institutional repositories are notoriously known to hold mostly material donated by or about white people. This situation, I felt, proved that reality. Nevertheless, I was still able to gain some of the other skills I was looking for during this rotation. I was able to process a collection using ArchivesSpace and put together a finding aid that was then published online. I was also able to put together an exhibit at the library about a particular event in my institution's history in the 1950s. This rotation was extended extra time because there had not been formal structure put in place for a resident in the archives department, and for the first formal duration of my rotation, I had only been assigned the oral history guidelines project.

During this rotation, again, the feeling of not having institutional guidance was further demonstrated. Although I was assigned more projects than in Reference, I did not have very many opportunities to have vital conversations about how to get a job in the field. I remember, once the rotation was over, I had applied for a job at an archives for another institution. Even though I had shared my cover letter for this job with my rotation supervisor, they did not mention to me that a week later, they would be going to a workshop for ArchivesSpace taking place at that very institution. I wish they had shared with me that they were going so that I could have met people from that institution, which might have helped me in my job search.

I will say that it has been difficult now nearing the end of my term to be able to land a job. I was able to get one offer out of the fifteen applications that I submitted. This probably would not have been possible had it not been for this residency. In interviews it has been difficult for me to talk about a project as mine given the push back that I received when I tried to do that during the middle of my term at my institution. Still, I can claim having particular skills coupled with unique experiences as a result.

If other residency programs are anything like mine, then I have plenty of critique as demonstrated in the paragraphs above. Residency programs have to involve staff with a genuine interest in the advancement of the resident. They also need to take into serious consideration what the resident is looking to get out of the term. Lastly, they need to prepare the resident to have vital conversations pertaining to the branches of the field that they are applying to work in. Perhaps this is why many librarians of color leave the profession or why we lack representation in the field. It helped for me to stay connected with organizations and committees in the greater profession to feel at home with other librarians of color in the field. It also helped me to actively participate in diversity initiatives outside of my rotations to remind myself why it is important that I stay in this field. Serving as the advisor for a student group on campus, I had plenty of my students approach me at the reference desk asking for help with their papers outside of their meetings. I also had the opportunity to conduct instruction sessions for visiting scholars from a nearby community college as part of my institution's diversity recruitment efforts. Involvement in ways such as these were constant reminders that my presence was appreciated by my academic community.

With a month left of my residency, in retrospect, I was still glad to have been at my institution and to have been able to make the impact that I did. I hope that the skills I am walking away with will be marketable and will help me continue on this career path. I also hope that whomever the next resident is at my institution will be provided with more care and be listened to and will tailor the program to match their needs over the two-year term.

⊚ Key Points

- Coordinate institutional, library, and departmental orientations to avoid repetition and information overload.
- Take concrete steps to understand and ameliorate new job stress as part of onboarding, particularly stressors rooted in role ambiguity and time pressures.
- Set up regular support mechanisms during onboarding for the resident, including regular check-ins and opportunities for formal and informal mentorship. Support should include the resident's input and provide iterative opportunities to reflect on experiences over time.
- Support the resident's research and professional development by providing mentorship in the development of their research agenda and in selecting and navigating conferences and presentations.
- To ensure that diversity residencies make an impact in organizational efforts toward inclusion, take every opportunity to reflect on the norms of your workplace culture. Make efforts to ensure that they make room for the lived realities and experiences of your residents.

⊚ Notes

1. Mark Stein and Lilith Christiansen, *Successful Onboarding: A Strategy to Unlock Hidden Value Within Your Organization* (Maidenhead: McGraw-Hill, 2010).

2. Jolie O. Graybill et al., "Employee Onboarding: Identification of Best Practices in ACRL Libraries," *Library Management* 34, no. 3 (2013): 200–218, doi:https://doi.org/10.1108/01435121311310897.

3. Howard J. Klein, Beth Polin, and Kyra Leigh Sutton, "Specific Onboarding Practices for the Socialization of New Employees: Onboarding Practices," *International Journal of Selection and Assessment* 23, no. 3 (September 2015): 263–83, doi:10.1111/ijsa.12113.

4. Jen-te Yang, "Facilitating or Inhibiting Newcomer Socialisation Outcomes in International Hotels," *Tourism and Hospitality Research* 9, no. 4 (October 2009): 325–39, doi:10.1057/thr.2009.17; Rohit Verma, "Navigating Uncharted Waters," *Cornell Hospitality Quarterly* 53, no. 1 (February 2012): 4, doi:10.1177/1938965511430798.

5. Stacey Edmonson, "Role Ambiguity," *Encyclopedia of Educational Leadership and Administration* (Thousand Oaks, Cal.: SAGE Publications, 2006).

6. Sajni Lacey and Melanie Parlette-Stewart, "Jumping into the Deep: Imposter Syndrome, Defining Success and the New Librarian," *Partnership: The Canadian Journal of Library and Information Practice and Research* 12, no. 1 (August 23, 2017), doi:10.21083/partnership.v12i1.3979.

7. Sylvia S. Hu and Demetria E. Patrick, "Our Experience as Minority Residents: Benefits, Drawbacks, and Suggestions," *College & Research Libraries News* 67, no. 5 (May 1, 2006): 297–300, doi:10.5860/crln.67.5.7620.

8. Yang, "Facilitating or Inhibiting Newcomer Socialisation Outcomes."

9. B. Gail Caldwell and Cam Caldwell, "Ten Classic Onboarding Errors—Violations of the HRM-Employee Relationship," *Business and Management Research* 5, no. 4 (December 2, 2016): 47, doi:10.5430/bmr.v5n4p47.

10. William K. Black and Joan M. Leysen, "Fostering Success: The Socialization of Entry-Level Librarians in ARL Libraries," *Journal of Library Administration* 36, no. 4 (January 20, 2002): 3–27, doi:10.1300/J111v36n04_02.

11. Teresa Y. Neely, "Assessing Diversity Initiatives: The ARL Leadership and Career Development Program," *Journal of Library Administration* 49, no. 8 (December 8, 2009): 811–35, doi:10.1080/01930820903396830.

12. Justin Reedy, "Creating a Research Agenda," *Inside Higher Ed*, May 20, 2009, www.insidehighered.com/advice/2009/05/20/creating-research-agenda.

13. Robert Tomaszewski and Karen I. MacDonald, "Identifying Subject-Specific Conferences as Professional Development Opportunities for the Academic Librarian," *The Journal of Academic Librarianship* 35, no. 6 (November 2009): 583–90, doi:10.1016/j.acalib.2009.08.006.

14. Rosina Alaimo, "Top Six Reasons to Attend a Conference," *Knowledge Quest* 33, no. 1 (October 9, 2004): 34–35.

15. Rachel Harrison, "Unique Benefits of Conference Attendance as a Method of Professional Development for LIS Professionals," *The Serials Librarian* 59, no. 3–4 (September 27, 2010): 263–70, doi:10.1080/0361526X.2010.489353.

16. Angela Galvan, "Soliciting Performance, Hiding Bias: Whiteness and Librarianship," *In the Library with the Lead Pipe*, June 3, 2015, www.inthelibrarywiththeleadpipe.org/2015/soliciting-performance-hiding-bias-whiteness-and-librarianship/.

17. Association of College and Research Libraries, Diversity Alliance, "ACRL Diversity Alliance FAQ," American Library Association, March 6, 2017, www.ala.org/acrl/issues/alliancefaq.

18. Todd Honma, "Trippin' Over the Color Line: The Invisibility of Race in Library and Information Studies," *InterActions: UCLA Journal of Education and Information Studies* 1, no. 2 (2005), escholarship.org/uc/item/4nj0w1mp; April Hathcock, "White Librarianship in Blackface: Diversity Initiatives in LIS," *In the Library with the Lead Pipe*, October 7, 2015, www.inthelibrarywiththeleadpipe.org/2015/lis-diversity/; Jennifer Vinopal, "The Quest for Diversity in Library Staffing: From Awareness to Action," *In the Library with the Lead Pipe*, January 13, 2016, www.inthelibrarywiththeleadpipe.org/2016/quest-for-diversity/; Antonia P. Olivas, "The Motivation of Underrepresented Minority Librarians to Lead," in *At the Helm: Leading Transformation: The Proceedings of the Association of College and Research Libraries 2017 Conference* (Baltimore, Md.: American Library Association, 2017), 613–36.

19. Chanelle Pickens and Ashleigh D. Coren, "Diversity Residency Programs: Strategies for a Collaborative Approach to Development," *Collaborative Librarianship* 9, no. 2 (2017): 6.

20. Vinopal, "The Quest for Diversity in Library Staffing."

21. Greig De Peuter, "Creative Economy and Labor Precarity: A Contested Convergence," *Journal of Communication Inquiry* 35, no. 4 (2011): 417–25.

22. Kyu-Man Han et al., "Precarious Employment Associated with Depressive Symptoms and Suicidal Ideation in Adult Wage Workers," *Journal of Affective Disorders* 218 (August 15, 2017): 201–9, doi:10.1016/j.jad.2017.04.049.

23. Selena Zhang and Daniyal Zuberi, "Evening the Keel: Measuring and Responding to Precarity in the Canadian Labour Economy," *Canadian Public Administration* 60, no. 1 (March 1, 2017): 28–47, doi:10.1111/capa.12206.

24. Leah F. Vosko, Martha Macdonald, and Iain Campbell, *Gender and the Contours of Precarious Employment* (London: Routledge, 2009).

25. Michael Krasman, "Three Must-Have Onboarding Elements for New and Relocated Employees," *Employment Relations Today* 42, no. 2 (July 2015): 9–14, doi:10.1002/ert.21493.

26. Adena Brons et al., "Precarity in Libraries," BC Library Conference, Richmond, British Columbia, May 10, 2018, https://osf.io/ybczx/.

References

Alaimo, Rosina. "Top Six Reasons to Attend a Conference." *Knowledge Quest* 33, no. 1 (October 9, 2004): 34–35.

Association of College and Research Libraries, Diversity Alliance. "ACRL Diversity Alliance FAQ." American Library Association, March 6, 2017. www.ala.org/acrl/issues/alliancefaq.

Black, William K., and Joan M. Leysen. "Fostering Success: The Socialization of Entry-Level Librarians in ARL Libraries." *Journal of Library Administration* 36, no. 4 (January 20, 2002): 3–27. doi:10.1300/J111v36n04_02.

Brons, Adena, Chloe Riley, Ean Henninger, and Crystal Yin. "Precarity in Libraries." Presented at the BC Library Conference, Richmond, British Columbia, May 10, 2018. osf.io/ybczx/.

Caldwell, B. Gail, and Cam Caldwell. "Ten Classic Onboarding Errors—Violations of the HRM-Employee Relationship." *Business and Management Research* 5, no. 4 (December 2, 2016): 47. doi:10.5430/bmr.v5n4p47.

De Peuter, Greig. "Creative Economy and Labor Precarity: A Contested Convergence." *Journal of Communication Inquiry* 35, no. 4 (2011): 417–25.

Edmonson, Stacey. "Role Ambiguity." *Encyclopedia of Educational Leadership and Administration*. Thousand Oaks, Cal.: SAGE Publications, 2006.

Galvan, Angela. "Soliciting Performance, Hiding Bias: Whiteness and Librarianship." *In the Library with the Lead Pipe*, June 3, 2015. www.inthelibrarywiththeleadpipe.org/2015/soliciting-performance-hiding-bias-whiteness-and-librarianship/.

Graybill, Jolie O., Maria Taesil Hudson Carpenter, Jerome Offord, Mary Piorun, and Gary Shaffer. "Employee Onboarding: Identification of Best Practices in ACRL Libraries." *Library Management* 34, no. 3 (2013): 200–18. doi:https://doi.org/10.1108/01435121311310897.

Han, Kyu-Man, Jisoon Chang, Eunsoo Won, Minsoo Lee, and Byung-Joo Ham. "Precarious Employment Associated with Depressive Symptoms and Suicidal Ideation in Adult Wage Workers." *Journal of Affective Disorders* 218 (August 15, 2017): 201–9. doi:10.1016/j.jad.2017.04.049.

Harrison, Rachel. "Unique Benefits of Conference Attendance as a Method of Professional Development for LIS Professionals." *The Serials Librarian* 59, no. 3–4 (September 27, 2010): 263–70. doi:10.1080/0361526X.2010.489353.

Hathcock, April. "White Librarianship in Blackface: Diversity Initiatives in LIS." *In the Library with the Lead Pipe*, October 7, 2015. www.inthelibrarywiththeleadpipe.org/2015/lis-diversity/.

Honma, Todd. "Trippin' Over the Color Line: The Invisibility of Race in Library and Information Studies." *InterActions: UCLA Journal of Education and Information Studies* 1, no. 2 (2005). escholarship.org/uc/item/4nj0w1mp.

Hu, Sylvia S., and Demetria E. Patrick. "Our Experience as Minority Residents: Benefits, Drawbacks, and Suggestions." *College & Research Libraries News* 67, no. 5 (May 1, 2006): 297–300. doi:10.5860/crln.67.5.7620.

Klein, Howard J., Beth Polin, and Kyra Leigh Sutton. "Specific Onboarding Practices for the Socialization of New Employees: Onboarding Practices." *International Journal of Selection and Assessment* 23, no. 3 (September 2015): 263–83. doi:10.1111/ijsa.12113.

Krasman, Michael. "Three Must-Have Onboarding Elements for New and Relocated Employees." *Employment Relations Today* 42, no. 2 (July 2015): 9–14. doi:10.1002/ert.21493.

Lacey, Sajni, and Melanie Parlette-Stewart. "Jumping into the Deep: Imposter Syndrome, Defining Success and the New Librarian." *Partnership: The Canadian Journal of Library and Information Practice and Research* 12, no. 1 (August 23, 2017). doi:10.21083/partnership.v12i1.3979.

Neely, Teresa Y. "Assessing Diversity Initiatives: The ARL Leadership and Career Development Program." *Journal of Library Administration* 49, no. 8 (December 8, 2009): 811–35. doi:10.1080/01930820903396830.

Olivas, Antonia P. "The Motivation of Underrepresented Minority Librarians to Lead." In *At the Helm: Leading Transformation: The Proceedings of the Association of College and Research Libraries 2017 Conference*, 613–36. Baltimore, Md.: American Library Association, 2017.

Park, Hannah Lee. "Residency Autoethnography," September 5, 2018.

Pickens, Chanelle, and Ashleigh D. Coren. "Diversity Residency Programs: Strategies for a Collaborative Approach to Development." *Collaborative Librarianship* 9, no. 2 (2017): 6.

Reedy, Justin. "Creating a Research Agenda." *Inside Higher Ed*, May 20, 2009. www.insidehigher ed.com/advice/2009/05/20/creating-research-agenda.

Stein, Mark, and Lilith Christiansen. *Successful Onboarding: A Strategy to Unlock Hidden Value Within Your Organization*. Maidenhead: McGraw-Hill, 2010.

Tomaszewski, Robert, and Karen I. MacDonald. "Identifying Subject-Specific Conferences as Professional Development Opportunities for the Academic Librarian." *The Journal of Academic Librarianship* 35, no. 6 (November 2009): 583–90. doi:10.1016/j.acalib.2009.08.006.

Verma, Rohit. "Navigating Uncharted Waters." *Cornell Hospitality Quarterly* 53, no. 1 (February 2012): 4. doi:10.1177/1938965511430798.

Vinopal, Jennifer. "The Quest for Diversity in Library Staffing: From Awareness to Action." *In the Library with the Lead Pipe*, January 13, 2016. /www.inthelibrarywiththeleadpipe.org/2016/quest-for-diversity/.

Vosko, Leah F., Martha Macdonald, and Iain Campbell. *Gender and the Contours of Precarious Employment*. London: Routledge, 2009.

Yang, Jen-te. "Facilitating or Inhibiting Newcomer Socialisation Outcomes in International Hotels." *Tourism and Hospitality Research* 9, no. 4 (October 2009): 325–39. doi:10.1057/thr.2009.17.

Zhang, Selena, and Daniyal Zuberi. "Evening the Keel: Measuring and Responding to Precarity in the Canadian Labour Economy." *Canadian Public Administration* 60, no. 1 (March 1, 2017): 28–47. doi:10.1111/capa.12206.

CHAPTER 9

Developing an Assessment Plan for the Residency

IN THIS CHAPTER

▷ Defining Assessment and Evaluation

▷ Types of Assessment

▷ Feminist and Critical Assessment

▷ Planning Effective Assessment

A S EARLIER CHAPTERS SUGGESTED, residencies can provide benefits to the profession, the institution, and the resident, as well as other stakeholders. However, in order to understand the impact of these benefits compared to the cost of resources invested, assessing and evaluating multiple elements of the residency program is useful. In many cases, it can be tempting for residency planners, such as the residency coordinator, to focus on the development of the program and skip planning assessment. However, this approach is often risky, leaving the resident and stakeholders with little more than a vague sense of what went well and what did not. Failing to incorporate formative assessment throughout the residency life cycle also means that evaluators run the risk of missing opportunities for improvement throughout the residency. In our research, five out of the nine residency coordinators who responded and eleven out of the sixteen residents who responded indicated that their residency had no formal assessment program. Although from a very small sample, these examples suggest that many residencies may struggle to create and use assessment and evaluation plans. This chapter will focus on describing assessment, exploring how it can be used in a residency program to inform decision making, and suggesting strategies and tactics for planning assessments.

◎ Defining Assessment and Evaluation

There are many definitions of assessment and evaluation, and the two terms are often used interchangeably. However, for the purposes of this chapter, we define assessment as the process of identifying and collecting data about an activity. Evaluation is the process of using this data to make a decision about how well the initial objectives for the activity were met. Therefore, assessment enables evaluation, helping organizations determine what elements of an activity are meeting their objectives and which parts need to be changed.

Consider the cases below. In each of these cases, evaluations and assessments can provide data that enables program stakeholders to make decisions about areas for improvement.

- LaToya is the lead for a project that her library's resident is working on that involves metadata development and standardization. She assigns the resident a project involving Dublin Core metadata standards. Before the work begins, she and the resident pinpoint how the resident will demonstrate that he can use these standards effectively. Then, when the resident is finished with the project, he shows LaToya the work and explains how it meets each of the standards they decided on.
- Hiroko is the associate dean at her library and is responsible for allotting professional development money. She wonders how much money she should allot for the incoming resident. She consults with several other residency program planners through a listserv to learn more about how they decide to apportion money and follows their best practices.
- This year, Pat designed a survey for past residents asking them questions about how soon they got a library job after completing their residency, whether they are still employed in librarianship, and whether the residency taught them skills they use in the jobs today. They compiled this data and presented it to the director of the library in order to demonstrate that most residents had gotten jobs more quickly than average after completing the program, are still librarians, and still use information they learned in the residency. Based on these findings, the library decided to continue funding the project.

Each scenario represents a situation when evidence or data can help stakeholders solve problems and make decisions. Having evidence, rather than relying on gut feelings or subjective impressions, enables stakeholders to make better decisions about how to allocate resources such as time and money and provides evidence about how programs support the library's mission.[1] Another major benefit of planning assessment and evaluation in advance is that it enables stakeholders to come to an agreement about appropriate assessment measures, encouraging consistency if multiple evaluators are involved. Clarifying assessments ahead of time enables residents and those supporting them to course correct if they feel they will not be able to meet the assessment criteria.[2]

◎ Types of Assessment

There are two major types of assessment: formative and summative. Formative assessment occurs before and during a program, enabling internal stakeholders to adjust and reassess the program or specific elements of it. Formative assessments "are typically conducted during development of a program or its ongoing operation" in order to provide "feedback for improvement."[3] Formative assessments and evaluations conducted during the course of a resident's time at your library have the benefit of allowing the current resident to actually reap the benefits of assessment-informed programmatic changes during his or her cycle, as opposed to merely providing the input that improves the experience of the next resident. In contrast, summative assessments evaluate the program as a whole in order to "convey a cumulative record of what was done and accomplished." Its purpose can be to evaluate whether the program met outcomes. Hernon notes that "results from external evaluations, when conveyed in reports, inform stakeholders about how well the library meets the needs and expectations of constituent groups and other stakeholders while aligning services and programs with the institution's mission and goals."[4] Throughout the residency, you will want to incorporate both formative and cumulative assessment.

There are also multiple types of assessment data that may be useful in assessments. Although there are many nuances to types of data, they can be broken down in their most basic level to quantitative, qualitative, and mixed-methods data. Quantitative data usually includes numbers-based data and answers questions about characteristics or specific measurements of program outcomes. For example, questions best answered with quantitative data might be: How many residents has the program had? How many people participated in a specific outreach program? On the other hand, qualitative data deals more with perceptions of information and is often text-based. This kind of information is more useful for gathering perceptions of information. In many cases, assessors combine quantitative and qualitative data collection methods to practice mixed-methods research. Mixed-methods assessment can be useful because it allows assessors to get multiple kinds of data to answer a question.

In some cases, multiple types of data are gathered in a single assessment tool. For instance, a survey may ask several questions that assign numerical responses but also have open boxes for participants to share their impressions of a program, which is a qualitative response. Determining the kind of data you want to get back (a number or a textual description) can help decide which kinds of assessment measures to use.

Once you have determined what kind of assessment is necessary and what behaviors you plan to assess, you can determine or develop the best kind of tool for the assessment. There are multiple tools available, many of which you have likely used in other scenarios. Here are some examples that may be useful:

- Performance/observation: Observing a person completing a task in order to determine whether or not the task was completed appropriately.
- Questionnaires: Asking a person to rank their satisfaction with a program or which elements of a program were most useful.
- Survey questionnaires: Asking a group of people, such as prior residents, about their satisfaction with a program.
- Interviews: Asking residents, supervisors, or other stakeholders for in-depth feedback about their experiences.
- Rubrics: Asking residents to assess themselves or others on a graduated list demonstrating basic skill to advanced skill.
- Checklists: Asking residents to demonstrate or indicate they can do all of the parts of a process.
- Reflections: Asking residents, supervisors, or other stakeholders to reflect in writing about their experiences.

EXAMPLE SELF-ASSESSMENT SURVEY FOR THE RESIDENT ABOUT SERVING ON THE REFERENCE DESK

How comfortable to do you feel . . .

1. Answering directional questions (i.e., where is the bathroom?) at the reference desk?

1	2	3	4	5
Cannot do this at all	Very uncomfortable	Uncomfortable	Comfortable	Very comfortable

   Comments:

2. Answering printing questions (i.e., how can I print my document?) at the reference desk?

1	2	3	4	5
Cannot do this at all	Very uncomfortable	Uncomfortable	Comfortable	Very comfortable

   Comments:

3. Answering questions about finding materials (i.e., where can I find a book with a known title?) at the reference desk?

1	2	3	4	5
Cannot do this at all	Very uncomfortable	Uncomfortable	Comfortable	Very comfortable

   Comments:

4. Answering basic research questions (i.e., where can I begin research in my topic?) at the reference desk?

1	2	3	4	5
Cannot do this at all	Very uncomfortable	Uncomfortable	Comfortable	Very comfortable

   Comments:

5. Making referrals for advanced research questions (i.e., who is the engineering librarian?) at the reference desk?

1	2	3	4	5
Cannot do this at all	Very uncomfortable	Uncomfortable	Comfortable	Very comfortable

   Comments:

Table 9.1. Sample Evaluation Rubric for Resident

LEARNING OBJECTIVE	BASIC	SUFFICIENT	EXCELLENT
Resident will be able to describe the functions of Special Collections, particularly its internal structure and how it works with other departments in the library, in order to understand Special Collections' role in the library and how different departments work together to serve patrons effectively.	Resident can provide a generic description of the functions of a Special Collections department.	Resident can provide a clear description of the functions of Special Collections and how it works with other departments.	Resident can describe the workflow of each of the divisions in Special Collections and how other departments participate in that workflow.
Resident can apply appropriate metadata and description for individual collections in Special Collections, demonstrating the ability to apply metadata principles in a future position.	Resident can explain the process of applying metadata and creating descriptive materials, like EAD finding aids, for a collection.	Resident can apply metadata effectively to a collection.	Resident can create an EAD access tool if needed and describe how to do a metadata crosswalk.
Resident can complete the process of converting analog objects into digital items to be accessed and preserved, including digitization, metadata, preservation, and display in order to show they have the skills necessary to participate in similar projects in another position.	Resident can describe how to complete the process of converting analog objects into digital items.	Resident can digitize, create metadata, and provide preservation and display for items with help and prompting from area advisor.	Resident can digitize, create metadata, and provide preservation and display for items independently.

Assessment in Residencies

There are multiple points throughout the residency when assessments are useful:

- Learning assessment and evaluation: Regular assessment to determine if the resident is meeting learning outcomes enables shifts in learning activities and planning. These assessments might also include gathering feedback from residents, supervisors, and project planners.
- Program assessment and evaluation: Assessing specific elements of your program can enable you to see areas that are going well and areas where more growth would be useful. For example, evaluating how many residents have gone on to get jobs in libraries and during what time frame might be useful.
- Stakeholder assessment and evaluation: Assessing the performance of coordinators, project or area advisors, or assigned mentors is a good way to determine if these stakeholders are meeting performance objectives.

◎ Feminist and Critical Assessment

> "Feminist assessment is inherently reflexive, and reflection itself is a feminist act."[9]

Assessment and evaluation should provide information that benefits the institution, the resident, and the other stakeholders. Evaluation can be an important opportunity for the resident to examine his or her own progress and get feedback from others. Allowing the resident to participate in the process gives all of the stakeholders equal footing. It is also important to begin this process planning early so both the resident and the other stakeholders have time to put a useful plan in place. Pickens and Coren suggest that "specific measures for evaluation should be created early in the design of a residency program. . . . Experiences of residents will vary, so assessing these early in the program will allow space for modification if necessary.[5]

One approach to consider when developing assessment is to adopt a critical perspective. Feminist assessment comes from the field of feminist pedagogy, which aims to replace traditional forms of assessment that favor hierarchy with models that allow the resident to participate as an equal.[6] Instead of invoking a power hierarchy where the resident is at the bottom and the supervisor is the authority, this model privileges the agency of the resident.[7] Feminist assessment, like feminist pedagogy, decenters the teacher (or supervisor, in our case) and their authority in order to include the student (or resident) in the assessment of her own experience; "it is learner-centered and diverse and validates differing perspectives and voices. It challenges the power relations that govern traditional assessment methods."[8] And instead of existing only to benefit stakeholders, the institution, or the program, the assessment benefits the resident by helping them shape their own growth and measure their own accomplishments.

There are multiple ways to apply these concepts in the residency program:

- Involve the resident in setting the learning goals or competencies and the assessments for her projects.
- Explain to the resident when assessments will occur and how they will be used.
- Give the resident multiple opportunities to reflect and solicit feedback on her performance in a supportive environment.
- Plan assessment activities that are helpful for the resident, not just other stakeholders.
- Provide the resident with opportunities to reflect on her growth. For example, consider having your resident keep a diary that acts as a log of not only her work but how she feels about the work she has accomplished.

◎ Planning Effective Assessment

In order to apply assessment effectively, it is important to be very clear about the focus of the assessment. Having a clear set of outcomes is necessary for assessment to be effective, as chapter 4 explained. If the required outcome is unclear, no assessment will be able to measure it appropriately. Thus, the process is best done in conjunction with or after developing program or learning outcomes and activities. Consider this example professional objective: Resident will be able to apply appropriate metadata standards. Initially, this behavioral objective seems to suggest that the appropriate assessment would be to observe the resident applying metadata standards. However, such a learning objective and assessment would benefit from clarifying a number of questions. First, we should determine what specific behavior we expect the resident to demonstrate to indicate that they can apply standards. Will they be able to create original metadata using a specific set of standards? Will they be able to recognize a specific standard in use when reviewing a metadata record? Will they be able to use a specific tool to update metadata? Since it is unlikely the resident will learn all standards equally well, do we expect them to use a specific standard? To what kinds of objects or information should they be able to apply the standard? In addition, we should clarify when we expect the resident to learn these skills. Should the resident be able to perform after a specific project or training session, or should we expect the resident to acquire this skill before they leave the institution? If we expect the resident to perform this task by the end of a project, then the assessment should occur once the project is complete. If we expect the resident to learn skills along the way and apply them, then assessment should occur regularly throughout the project.

The same rigorous process should also be applied to program or stakeholder evaluations. For instance, institutions should decide ahead of time when they will collect feedback and from whom. For program evaluation, this might be making a plan to follow up with previous residents about how quickly they got jobs, whether they stayed in librarianship, or whether they perceive that participating in the program improved their career success. One might also ask residents to rank the most helpful and least helpful elements of the program, planning in advance which elements to include in the assessment and evaluation. The same is true for stakeholders. Since assessing a supervisor directly with that supervisor might be difficult for a resident given the power dynamic, perhaps an HR professional or senior colleague would agree at the start of the residency to regularly gather feedback from the resident, any project or area coordinators, or other stakeholders about specific areas of performance to share with the supervisor at regular intervals.

One good way to stay on track with assessments and evaluations is to develop an assessment and evaluation data collection plan. The plan should include your timeline for collecting the data, who will be the study participant or subject of the data gathering, what kind of data will be collected, and what the methodology will be for collecting the data.

Once you have this information, the next important step is to consider how you can use it to maximize what is going well and make changes where necessary. For example, if feedback shows that a resident or supervisor is struggling with a specific kind of issue, this may be the time to provide additional training or a mentor in this area. If residents are having trouble getting jobs after the program, this might be an opportunity to consider how the program prepares residents for their future endeavors. Although planning assessment takes work, thinking ahead of time about what components of the program you want to measure and the best kind of data to measure them enables the process to flow smoothly. By developing an assessment plan, your institution can determine what is going well in the residency and what areas might need changes.

Table 9.2. Sample Data Collection Plan for Assessment

TIMELINE	STUDY PARTICIPANTS	DATA TYPE	METHODOLOGY
60 days before residency begins	resident	in-person interview	Supervisor will interview the resident to learn more about their interests in librarianship. This data will be used to finalize resident projects.
every two weeks	area advisor and resident		Area advisors/project coordinators will observe and evaluate the resident's skill in meeting each of the project learning goals.
every 30 days	resident resident and supervisor	blog questionnaire with short answers included	Resident will keep a reflective blog of their experiences. Resident and supervisor will both fill out a questionnaire about their own and each other's performance. Assessment team will be analyzing questionnaire and blog text for emerging themes.

Table 9.3. Data Collection Plan Template

TIMELINE	STUDY PARTICIPANTS	DATA TYPE	METHODOLOGY	

Questions to consider when planning assessments:

- When should the objective be complete? Should the objective be met at the end of an onboarding period, the end of a project, or the end of the program? Deciding when the objective should be met enables you to determine when the assessment should be done.
- Is the objective one that is learned on a continuum, or is it a yes or no objective? Some types of objectives require yes or no criteria: Did the resident get a job within six months of the residency's completion? Did the resident present or publish scholarly work? In these cases, an assessment that focuses on a yes/no answer is appropriate. Other kinds of objectives, however, require assessment along a continuum. For example, how well a resident can describe a process might best be measured along a continuum using a tool like a rubric.
- What specific behavior or visible change will we expect to see that signifies meeting the outcome? For example, will the resident be able to identify a certain kind of object, to implement a program, or to complete a certain kind of work? Determining how we will know if success is present is an important part of assessment.

Key Points

- Assessment is an important way to make decisions about the effectiveness of the residency using data.
- Developing effective assessments requires having clear learning objectives against which to measure.
- There are multiple types of assessment useful in different circumstances and multiple assessment tools. Choosing the correct type of assessment and the correct tool depends on what you want to measure.
- Assessment is only useful if it is used to either improve areas of the program or to verify and validate what is working well.

Notes

1. Meredith Gorran Farkas, "Building and Sustaining a Culture of Assessment: Best Practices for Change Leadership," *Reference Services Review* 41, no. 1 (2013): 13–31.

2. Grant P. Wiggins and Jay McTighe, *The Understanding by Design Guide to Advanced Concepts in Creating and Reviewing Units* (Alexandria, Va.: Association for Supervision and Curriculum Development, 2012).

3. Daniel L. Stufflebeam and Chris L. S. Coryn, *Evaluation Theory, Models, and Applications*, 2nd ed. (San Francisco, Cal.: Jossey-Bass, 2014), 21.

4. Peter Hernon, Robert E. Dugan, and Joseph R. Matthews, *Getting Started with Evaluation* (Chicago: American Library Association, 2014), 63.

5. Chanelle Pickens and Ashleigh D. Coren, "Diversity Residency Programs: Strategies for a Collaborative Approach to Development," *Collaborative Librarianship* 9, no. 2 (2017): 105.

6. Carolyn M. Shrewsbury, "What Is Feminist Pedagogy?," *Women's Studies Quarterly* 21, no. 3/4 (1993): 8–16.

7. Maria T. Accardi, *Feminist Pedagogy for Library Instruction* (Sacramento, Cal.: Litwin Books, 2013).

8. Ibid., 76.

9. Accardi, *Feminist Pedagogy for Library Instruction*.

◎ References

Accardi, Maria T. *Feminist Pedagogy for Library Instruction.* Sacramento, Cal.: Litwin Books, 2013.

Gorran Farkas, Meredith. "Building and Sustaining a Culture of Assessment: Best Practices for Change Leadership." *Reference Services Review* 41, no. 1 (2013): 13–31.

Hernon, Peter, Robert E. Dugan, and Joseph R. Matthews. *Getting Started with Evaluation.* Chicago: American Library Association, 2014.

Pickens, Chanelle, and Ashleigh D. Coren. "Diversity Residency Programs: Strategies for a Collaborative Approach to Development." *Collaborative Librarianship* 9, no. 2 (2017): 7.

Shrewsbury, Carolyn M. "What Is Feminist Pedagogy?" *Women's Studies Quarterly* 21, no. 3/4 (1993): 8–16.

Stufflebeam, Daniel L., and Chris L. S. Coryn. *Evaluation Theory, Models, and Applications.* 2nd ed. San Francisco, Cal.: Jossey-Bass, 2014.

Wiggins, Grant P., and Jay McTighe. *The Understanding by Design Guide to Advanced Concepts in Creating and Reviewing Units.* Alexandria, Va.: Association for Supervision and Curriculum Development, 2012.

CHAPTER 10

How Can I Support My Resident After the Residency?

S O YOU HAVE SUCCESSFULLY HOSTED a resident. Congratulations! But now what? As stated earlier, the purpose of most academic residency programs is to not only diversify the workforce but also to give new career professionals the experience they need to launch a successful career after the residency. Your job as a residency program stakeholder does not end when your resident leaves. So how do you support them? Some major areas where residents may need additional support during the end stages and after the residency include job hunting and mentoring support.

One of the challenges for new professionals is the job hunt, which occurs both in graduate school and the residency. Since job advertisements are written to allow for multiple applicants to show how their knowledge, skills, and abilities meet the organizational requirements, applicants may be uncertain if their skills are exactly what the organization needs. This uncertainty, combined with anxiety over potential rejection, might make residents feel very stressed. The job hunt also takes up a lot of time and energy in addition to the demands of completing the residency or preparing to relocate for a new position. Supporting the resident through this process not only will help them find that dream job to launch their career, but it will set them up for success when they move on from that position to bigger and brighter things.

And your relationship with your resident does not have to end just because their contracted time is over. You as their coordinator and supervisor have helped them to navigate academia, professional communication, research, and everything else that being a librarian entails. You are aware of her strengths and weaknesses, her aspirations, even her personal struggles. You are therefore in a perfect position to continue your relationship as a mentor, especially as she transitions from the residency to her career.

Job Hunting Support

Before you can help your resident after the residency, they first need to get a job in which to transition. It is likely they will have recently gone through this process since residencies at most last three years and start within a year or two of finishing a graduate program; the thought of going through that again can already seem exhausting and stressful. You can help reduce that stress by helping them look for jobs, decode job ads, prepare supporting documents, prepare for interviews, and network.

Places to Look

In our Internet age, we can look for jobs all over the world, in every type of library. Although this drastically improves our chances of finding the job that suits us best, it also gives us so many options that it can be hard to know where to start. The first step in helping your resident find a job is showing her where to look for jobs and how to be specific when searching.

When looking for jobs, it is not uncommon to subscribe to several different websites and listservs. Subscribing to websites via RSS feeds and listservs is a great way to narrow your focus and keep out unwanted job ads. To help your resident choose sources, talk about what sort of job they want. Are they interested in public services or technical services? Does he want to stay in academia? If so, what kind of institution? Does she want to live in a certain area? Does tenure or faculty status matter to him? Based on the job your resident wants, not only can you help her prioritize search sites, but you can help her develop a search strategy just like you would in a reference interview.

Finally, you need to reassure your resident that she is allowed to only apply for jobs she wants, not just every job for which she qualifies. Depending on a person's background, socioeconomic status, or marginalization, they might either feel she has to accept whatever job comes along, just in case, or they might have very reasonable fears about moving to and working in certain parts of the country. Your resident should feel safe and confident about where they apply and interviewing. Perhaps relate stories of times you have refused job offers or ignored job postings. Another good idea would be to help them research human rights legislation and cultural attitudes across the country. You might be surprised at what you learn.

Decoding Job Ads

How many times have you read a job ad and weren't quite sure exactly what kind of position they were hiring for or even exactly what kind candidate they wanted? Probably a lot, right? We have a habit as librarians of thinking that the language or format we use is universally understood. This of course is not the case. It can be helpful to sit down with your resident and go through job ads line by line to make sure every part of the ad is understood and if not who to contact. For example, many job ads use *supervise*, *manage*, and

Table 10.1. Compiled List of Job Searching Websites and Resources

ALL LIBRARY JOBS	PUBLIC LIBRARIES	ACADEMIC LIBRARIES	GOVERNMENT LIBRARIES	SPECIAL LIBRARIES	ARCHIVES	MUSEUMS
ALA JobList: joblist.ala.org	Public library websites	The Chronicle of Higher Education (ChronicleVitae): chroniclevitae.com	USAJobs: www.usajobs.gov	Special Libraries Association Job List: careers.sla.org/jobs/	Society of American Archivists Career Center: careers.archivists.org/jobs	American Alliance of Museums jobHQ: aam-us-jobs.careerwebsite.com/jobs/
INALJ (I Need a Library Job): inalj.com		HigherEdJobs: www.higheredjobs.com	GovernmentJobs: governmentjobs.com	Special library websites	Archives websites	Museum Employment Resource Center: museum-employment.com
Library Crossing: www.librarycrossing.com		Academic library websites	CareerOneStop: careeronestop.org/JobSearch/job-search.aspx			Museum Jobs: museum.jobs
State library associations			Government library websites			Museum websites
Job aggregate websites like Monster and Indeed						
Listservs of professional organizations, particularly those that cater to job type rather than type of library						

lead almost interchangeably even though they have subtle differences in meaning. When searching through the library literature for guidelines when using these terms, none is to be found. If in doubt, do not hesitate to have your resident contact the institution for clarification. After all, the job ad *should* have a contact person for such questions.

Since you have probably been on a search committee or two (especially the committee for your resident), you have some knowledge as to how we write job ads. Let your resident get a peek behind the curtain, so to speak, or even have them serve on a search committee for the next resident(s). Serving on search committees allows your resident to take part in every step of the hiring process, and this experience will give her insight into what makes a good candidate to a committee.

Supporting Documents Help

Every job your resident applies to will request these two documents: a resume/curriculum vitae (CV) and a cover letter. Encourage your residents to send you drafts of these documents for each job they apply to so that they know if they are adequately addressing everything in the ad and representing themselves accurately. Help them phrase their skills and job duties to make them seem like they are the perfect candidate for that position (because of course they are!) and maybe even show them your CV so that they can see what one should look like.

Beau Steenken, a law librarian, recommends two approaches to crafting the CV. The first is to "draft a master list of your experiences, skills, educational achievements, activities, etc." and match these to the list of qualities desired by each position. The second is to shift and reorder CV items to fit each position. For instance, for "tenure-track positions, masters' theses and involvement in university committees" are located higher and more prominently in the document.[1]

> Encourage your residents to write a "template" cover letter and CV that they can then tailor for each ad.

Websites and Portfolios

Due to the nature of residency positions—and being a recent graduate—your resident likely has several projects that would be of interest to potential employers. There are several ways that you and your resident can showcase their hard work during the job hunt and beyond, mainly in the form of websites and online portfolios.

To show the full extent of their work and interests, your resident might consider crafting a website. This could take the form of a blog on your library's website, or it could be a unique domain name purchased by the resident. Domain names are usually cheap, and hosting sites like WordPress, Weebly, Wix, and SquareSpace often allow you to purchase domain names through them; these sites also walk you through website construction. Your resident can make pages dedicated to instruction, to projects, and even to research interests. This gives potential employers more context than cover letters and CVs.

If your resident does more publishing and presenting, or other forms of output that aren't as easily displayed visually, have them set up an ORCID to list their research or perhaps a GitHub to display coding and metadata. These sites have the advantage of being designed as places to host data and bibliographies rather than visual projects or large text descriptions, and your resident can continue to build on them throughout their career at no cost.

Mock Interviews

Interviewing is exhausting. We know this, especially in academia where the final interview is an all-day process. The more prepared and relaxed your resident is when going through that process, the better. Give them examples of questions they might be asked based on your own experience and have them speak with people in your library who have jobs similar to the ones to which the resident applies. Train them how to structure an answer, especially when those answers are improvised (although it helps to have them construct answers for common questions). When structuring their answer, your resident could follow the STAR method: Situation, Task, Activity, and Result.[2] By using the STAR method, your resident can keep their answer specific and concise while still giving context and plenty of important details. This is another area where having your resident serve on a search committee will set them up for success, as they can then see the types of questions asked, why those questions are asked, and what committees look for in answers to those questions.

Networking

Your resident can have an advantage in the job hunting competition if she has successfully networked through the residency. Introduce your resident to your colleagues at other libraries. Encourage them to present or even just attend conferences. The more your resident makes a name for themself outside of your institution, the more feet in the door they'll have at those institutions.

Mentoring

It might seem obvious that effective mentoring sets your resident up for success after the residency, but it is worth investigating despite that. Of course, the very purpose of a residency program is to have formal mentoring during the first few years of a career. However, again, that mentorship does not have to end just because your resident leaves. You can in fact become a lifelong mentor for your resident!

During the Residency

As a residency coordinator, or even just as a supervisor or colleague, you are responsible in some way for mentoring the resident. You are established in your career and therefore provide an example for your resident, especially if your job duties are similar to what they want to do in their career. Mentoring during the residency will look different depending on your relationship to the resident, but it can either be informal or formal.

An important thing to keep in mind while mentoring your resident or residents, especially considering that they are early-career librarians and possibly members of marginalized groups, is the effect of psychosocial factors and how you can help to mitigate those effects. These factors can include racial microaggressions, imposter syndrome, and burnout. A 2017 study analyzed the library literature for discussions of library mentoring, and it found that "the LIS literature has tended to ignore or shy away from the more affective, personal aspects of mentoring." We argue that mentors, in addition to being advocates for the resident, can help the resident "make sense of their experiences."[3]

Formal Mentoring

Many library residency programs formally incorporate mentoring by assigning the resident an experienced librarian mentor who is separate from the supervisor. This mentor is somebody who is in the line of work the resident sees himself entering. Frequently, academic libraries will assign mentors to faculty members going through the tenure process in order to help them evaluate and organize their professional portfolios. Similarly, assigning a mentor (who is not the residency coordinator) to guide the resident through his career is crucial for success. The mentor is not only there to advise the resident in career-related issues, however; a mentor can be a trusted confidant when personal matters affect work matters, such as the death of a family member or financial problems.

A mentor and mentee should meet regularly, at least once a month, so that the resident has the opportunity to ask questions and share successes. The mentor should also feel comfortable asking questions of the resident, such as asking how certain projects are coming along or how he is working toward his current goals. A mentor could also ask how the resident is doing outside of work. Showing interest in a resident's life could help the resident feel comfortable coming to the mentor with serious issues, like mental or physical health problems.

Informal Mentoring

If you aren't the residency coordinator or the resident's assigned mentor, that doesn't mean you can't also offer your mentorship! Just by virtue of being in the profession longer, you are somebody that your resident can look up to for advice. You don't have to do as much as a formal mentor, but you can certainly offer your experience, your advice, and your connections to the resident to the best of your abilities.

After the Residency

Mentorship during the residency is of course important for setting the resident up for success later, but this chapter is really about what to do after. Unsurprisingly, mentorship *still plays a key role in success* after the resident moves on to bigger and better things. Although this can of course take the form of formal and informal mentoring, it also includes other venues.

Formal Mentoring

Although mentor programs that assign mentors to mentees are not as common outside of an institution, they do exist. In fact, several divisions and round tables of the American Library Association have formal mentorship programs that connect librarians across the nation. Make sure you make your resident aware of these programs during their residency so that they can more easily make that transition. These programs normally last a year, but of course, that relationship can continue in an informal way.

Informal Mentoring

You do not have to be assigned a mentee in order to fulfill the role of mentor. We all have people who have helped us get to where we are today, and to us, that is mentorship. Mentorship can be as complex as helping someone throughout their career or as simple as giving advice on Twitter. You can informally mentor your resident when they leave, or you can help them find others who can; in fact, you can help them find other mentors and still allow yourself to mentor them!

Open Communication

If a mentor/mentee relationship is not something you are willing or able to have with your resident once he leaves your institution, that does not mean that you have to cut off communication. Your resident should feel comfortable coming to you and others at your institution whenever they have questions, needs advice, or just wants to update you on how he is doing. Make sure that communication is open so that your resident can ask questions or request feedback.

Networking

A key part of mentoring and open communication is, of course, networking. If you see a call for participation that you think would be perfect for your former residents, send it their way! They will be glad that you thought of them. Continue to introduce your former residents to your colleagues and wider network of collaborators in the profession. Take them out to eat at conferences and invite other librarians along. Not only will this increase your former residents' professional networks, which of course is key in any career, but it will help them to feel more integrated into the profession with a sense of belonging.

Job hunting is not an easy task, especially when you have gone through the process only a year or two before doing it again. Your residents will need as much support as they can get from you and others to set them up for a career of success. Through the advice and suggestions in this book, you have created a program meant to nurture confident professionals. After they leave the program, further lend your support in appropriate capacities. Job hunting support and all forms of mentorship are crucial as your residents are preparing to advance in their career.

FINDING MY NETWORK: MENTORSHIP IN A LIBRARY RESIDENCY
by Hannah Lee Park

When I first told people that I had accepted a position in a two-year residency at the University of Delaware Library, and that I had turned down two other permanent positions for it, I remember the unspoken glances and questioning stares. Why would I turn down a permanent faculty position for something so temporary, and move across the country for it, no less? However, the job excited me in a way that the other job offers did not, and I was looking forward to tapping into my background and interests in multimodal composition, digital media, and librarianship while working at the Student Multimedia Design Center at UD. While the residency was quite established, having been created in 1984, it was the first time that my residency was based in one department; previous residencies had been on a rotational model. Soon after I had accepted the offer from UD, there was a call for nominations for the next convener of the Association of College and Research Libraries Residency Interest Group (RIG). Not quite knowing the full extent of what this would entail but wanting to get professionally involved, I volunteered and threw myself full force into this new adventure.

I had high hopes for the residency, but there were small bumps along the way. Because this was the first time the residency was based in one department, there was still a bit of figuring out the kinds of projects I wanted to work on and which units to collaborate with. There was also a coworker or two that looked upon me a bit warily, not quite sure what to make of me and what my role was to be in the department. In the midst of this, I also had to acclimate to the bureaucracy of working in an academic library and within higher education in general. It took a bit of maneuvering to navigate within the library's organizational culture, with its bureaucracy, hierarchy, and slowness to change—which is emblematic of large organizations in general. It was also a bit isolating being the only resident in the library, and I longed for another colleague who understood exactly what I was going through. I envied those residents who had a cohort of other residents that they could turn to and go through their residencies with.

I remember my first American Library Association (ALA) Midwinter Meeting, where I attended my first RIG meeting. In some ways, it felt like a homecoming. I had finally found my group of peers. There were residents from various universities across the country, and as we spoke about our experiences, there was a shared kinship that I hadn't felt with the more seasoned librarians at my university. The fact that we were all new to the profession, navigating academic libraries for the first time, with the added pressures of being from traditionally underrepresented groups in librarianship, helped us to connect on multiple levels. It was also helpful that several of these residents were at institutions that were within driving distance to the University of Delaware, so that we could engage with each other in person on a more regular basis.

Volunteering to be the incoming convener of RIG was a great stepping-stone into a leadership position, and it was a great way for me to get professionally involved. The experience was quite formative for me as I navigated through my residency. It provided me a safe network where I could brainstorm with others about possible areas for research, and together we wrote conference presentation proposals. Our proposal was accepted for the 2012 ALA Annual Conference, and we got together a group of residents, former residents, and residency coordinators to speak on "Winning on Two Fronts: How Library Residencies are Placing Libraries at the Leading Edge of Innovation and Diversity Initiatives." At the time, RIG had an even number of residents and residency coordinators who were active members, and the synergy of this mix helped move the group forward. The feedback from the other residency coordinators was quite valuable as we put together a grant proposal for the Association of College and Research Libraries Friends Fund. After a few rounds of revisions, RIG was awarded a grant to help send three residents to the second Joint Conference of Librarians of Color in 2012.

In some ways, RIG was like a guided mentorship on a group scale, with the added benefits of providing a built-in cohort. While I didn't have the fortune of being in a cohort-based residency at my institution, in some ways, RIG was my cohort. We were fellow residents, all early-career and navigating academic libraries for the first time, and even though we were at different institutions in different parts of the country, we could still relate on many levels. Among other things, RIG provided a way for us to write proposals for grants and presentations in a supportive environment, with the guidance of more seasoned residency coordinators. At the time, the leadership structure of RIG was such that a resident and a residency coordinator took turns being the convener of the group every other year. As the incoming convener, I learned much from the convener, who at the time was the residency coordinator at Towson University. However, it's my understanding that RIG consists of mostly residents now and that residency coordinators usually join ACRL's Diversity Alliance. It's been a while since I've been involved with residencies, so I don't know how this has changed the dynamic of the group. All I can say is that my time in RIG was invaluable.

While the University of Delaware Library provided a formal mentoring program, and while I was paired with another seasoned librarian for a semester, it was an external mentoring program that was my lifeline during certain parts of my career. I signed up to be a mentee for the ACRL Dr. E. J. Josey Mentoring Program for Spectrum Scholars, and I was matched with a library director of a small college in the Northeast. What should have lasted just one year has gone on seven years—and counting. During that time, we've had regularly scheduled phone conversations. It was during these conversations that I was finally able to completely open up about all the questions I had about what I was seeing in my library and university and the frustrations I had about certain policies and procedures and talk through the different issues I had as they came up.

I remember one particularly tumultuous time for me was when I was getting ready to put my dossier together for promotion. Toward the end of my residency, a permanent position opened up in my department, which I applied for and got. After working in this position for some time, I had the requisite number of years to go up for promotion. This was something that the HR librarian explained to me, and she encouraged me to submit my dossier for promotion. However, when I broached the topic with my supervisor, she said it was too early for me to go up for promotion—because she hadn't realized that my years as the resident would also count toward my promotion file. When I heard this, I remember feeling stunned. After some prompting, I was able to argue my case and submit my file. However, the experience left me shaken, and it was then that I realized just how much I had to advocate for myself and not take it for granted that others would do this for me. Talking through this experience with my mentor was immensely helpful, especially as she was an outsider observing the situation. There were countless other episodes like this, where I would experience something that left me questioning, and my mentor—with her decades of experience and rational, assuring voice—would give me the encouragement and confidence that I needed to know that my initial intuition to a particular situation was valid and that what I was observing or experiencing was something worth talking about. Although the mentoring relationship should have technically ended years ago, we're still in regular contact, and I'd like to imagine that we'll continue on in this mentoring relationship for many years to come. She keeps telling me that I have what it takes to take on more management and leadership roles in libraries. We'll see what the future holds. No matter where I eventually end up in my career, I'm thankful that I was given the chance to start my career in a residency.

⊚ Key Points

- The best way to support your residents after their residency is to set them up for success before they leave.
- As a professional, you can help your residents navigate the job hunting process.
- Mentoring should happen during the residency but can continue in a formal or informal way once your residents leave.

⊚ Notes

1. Beau Steenken, "How to Be Uncommon: Advice to Grads Seeking a First Professional Law Library Job from a Recent Survivor of the Process," *AALL Spectrum* 15 (2011): 19.

2. Michael Higgins, "Using the Star Technique to Shine at Job Interviews: A How-to Guide," *The Guardian*, March 10, 2014, sec. Guardian Careers, www.theguardian.com/careers/careers-blog/star-technique-competency-based-interview.

3. Bridget Farrell et al., "Addressing Psychosocial Factors with Library Mentoring," *Portal: Libraries and the Academy* 17, no. 1 (January 6, 2017): 55, doi:10.1353/pla.2017.0004.

⊚ References

Farrell, Bridget, Jaena Alabi, Pambanisha Whaley, and Claudine Jenda. "Addressing Psychosocial Factors with Library Mentoring." *Portal: Libraries and the Academy* 17, no. 1 (January 6, 2017): 51–69. doi:10.1353/pla.2017.0004.

Higgins, Michael. "Using the Star Technique to Shine at Job Interviews: A How-to Guide." *The Guardian*, March 10, 2014, sec. Guardian Careers. www.theguardian.com/careers/careers-blog/star-technique-competency-based-interview.

Steenken, Beau. "How to Be Uncommon: Advice to Grads Seeking a First Professional Law Library Job from a Recent Survivor of the Process." *AALL Spectrum* 15 (2011): 17–19.

⊚ Resources

"Huntr—Job Application Tracker." Accessed August 31, 2018. www.huntr.co.

"JibberJobber." Accessed August 31, 2018. www.jibberjobber.com/login.php.

"JobHero." JobHero. Accessed August 31, 2018. gojobhero.com.

"Library Jobs—ALA JobLIST | Jobs in Library & Information Science & Technology." Accessed August 31, 2018. joblist.ala.org/.

American Library Association. "Mentoring Opportunities." September 27, 2017. www.ala.org/educationcareers/mentoring-opportunities.

Hardenbrook, Joe. "Nailing the Library Interview." *Mr. Library Dude*, February 15, 2011. mrlibrarydude.wordpress.com/nailing-the-library-interview/.

Kelsky, Karen. "Dr. Karen's Rules of the Academic CV." *The Professor Is In*, August 19, 2016. theprofessorisin.com/2016/08/19/dr-karens-rules-of-the-academic-cv/.

Appendix A

2018–2019 List of Known Active Programs

Table A.1. Comprehensive Residency List Table

INSTITUTION	DIVERSITY ALLIANCE	LENGTH (IN YEARS)	NUMBER	COHORT	DIVERSITY	ROTATION	SINGLE	SUBJECT	LIBRARY TYPE	SUBJECTS
American University	1	2	1	0	0	0	1	1	Academic	Research, Teaching, and Learning
Bowling Green State University	1	3	1	0	1	1	1	0	Academic	
Clemson University	1	3	1	0	0	1	1	1	Academic	
Cornell University	0	2	1	0	1	1	1	0	Academic	
Florida State University	0	3	4	1	1	1	0	0	Academic	
Folger Shakespeare Library	0	0.75	1	0	0	0	1	1	Independent Research	Rare Materials
Grand Valley State University	1	3	1	0	0	0	1	1	Academic	Digital Projects and Services
Gulf Coast State College	0	3	1	0	0	1	1	0	Academic	
Harvard University	0	2	2	0	0	0	0	1	Academic	Changes with each residency
Indiana University Bloomington	1	3	1	0	1	1	0	1	Academic	
Iowa State University	1	3	1	0	0	1	0	0	Academic	Chosen by resident; Digital Scholarship and Initiatives, Library Instruction, Special Collections, and University Archives
L.A. as Subject	0	2	3	1	0	1	0	1	Academic; Archives	Archives
Library of Congress (Department Residencies)	0	0.5	4	1	0	0	0	1	Government	Acquisitions and Collection Development, Cataloging and Metadata, Collection Preservation, Reference and Instruction, Systems and Standards

Institution									Type	Focus
Library of Congress (National Digital Stewardship Residency)	0	1	5	1	0	0	1	1	Various	Digital Stewardship
Louisiana State University	1	2	1	0	0	1	1	0	Academic	
Loyola Marymount University	0	2	1	0	0	1	1	0	Academic	
Miami University (Oxford, OH)	0	1–2	1	0	1	0	1	1	Academic	Reference and Instruction
Michigan State University	0	3	1	0	0	0	1	1	Academic	Based on resident's interests
National Library of Medicine	0	1	5	1	0	0	0	1	Government	Health Sciences Librarianship
North Carolina State University	1	2	3	1	1	0	0	1	Academic	
Ohio State University	1	2	2	1	1	0	0	1	Academic	Digital Humanities, Cultural Diversity Inquiry
Pennsylvania State University	1	3	2	1	1	1	0	0	Academic	
Rutgers University	0	2 weeks	3	1	1	0	0	1	Archives	Jazz, African American History, Archives
Santa Barbara City College	0	0.75	1	0	0	1	0	0	Community College	
SUNY Geneseo	0	2	1	0	0	0	1	1	Academic	Research Instruction
SUNY Oswego	0	2	1	0	1	1	1	0	Academic	
SUNY Upstate	0	3	1	0	1	1	1	0	Academic	
Susquehanna University	1	3	1	0	1	0	1	1	Academic	Information Literacy, Digital Scholarship
Swarthmore College	1	2	1	0	1	0	1	1	Academic	Reference and Instruction
Syracuse University	0	2	1	0	1	0	1	1	Academic	Reference, Instruction, and Staff Training

(continued)

INSTITUTION	DIVERSITY ALLIANCE	LENGTH (IN YEARS)	NUMBER	COHORT	DIVERSITY	ROTATION	SINGLE	SUBJECT	LIBRARY TYPE	SUBJECTS
Temple University	0	2	1	0	1	1	1	0	Academic	
Texas A&M University	0	3	2	1	0	1	0	0	Academic	
Towson University	1	2	1	0	1	1	1	0	Academic	
University of Alberta	1	1	7	1	1	1	0	0	Academic	
University of California, Santa Barbara	0	2–3	1	0	0	1	1	0	Academic	
University of Chicago	0	2	3	1	0	0	0	1	Academic	Data Services, GIS, User Experience
University of Delaware	1	2	1	0	0	0	1	1	Academic	Subject changes with each residency
University of Denver	0	3	1	0	1	1	1	0	Academic	
University of Illinois at Urbana-Champaign (UIUC)	1	2	4	1	1	0	0	1	Academic	African American Studies, Data Visualization, Digital Humanities Pedagogy, Digital Preservation
University of Iowa	1	3	2	1	1	1	0	0	Academic	
University of Kansas	1	2	1	0	0	0	1	1	Academic	
University of Louisville	1	2	1	0	1	0	1	0	Academic	Research Assistance and Instruction
University of Massachusetts–Amherst	1	2	1	0	1	1	1	0	Academic	
University of Michigan	1	3	1–2	1	0	1	0	0	Academic	
University of Mississippi	0	2	1	0	0	1	1	0	Academic	
University of Nevada, Las Vegas	1	2	2	1	1	0	0	1	Academic	Digital Scholarship, Scholarly Communication

Institution									Type	
University of North Carolina, Greensboro	0	2	1	1	1	1	1	0	Academic	
University of Notre Dame	1	2–3	1	0	1	1	1	0	Academic	
University of Pennsylvania	1	3	1	0	0	0	1	1	Academic, STEM	STEM
University of Pittsburgh	0	2	1	0	1	1	0	0	Academic	
University of Tennessee, Knoxville	0	3	2	1	1	1	0	0	Academic	
University of Texas at Austin	0	2	2	1	1	1	1	0	Academic	
University of Texas at San Antonio	0	3	1	0	1	0	1	1	Academic	Student Success
University of Utah	1	2	1	0	1	1	1	0	Academic	
University of Virginia	0	3	2	1	1	1	0	1	Academic	Chosen by resident
University of Wisconsin, Madison	1	3	1	0	1	0	1	1	Academic	Chosen by resident
Valparaiso University	0	3	1	0	1	0	1	1	Academic	Scholarly Communications, Scholarly Publishing, Digital Humanities, and/or Copyright Services
Virginia Tech	1	3	1	0	1	1	1	0	Academic	
Western Michigan University	1	3	1	0	1	0	0	1	Academic	
Wayne State University	1	1–2	1	0	1	0	1	1	Academic	Reference, Instruction, Information Literacy
West Virginia University	1	3	2	1	1	1	0	0	Academic	
Yale University	0	3	2	0	0	0	0	1	Academic	Archives
	30			21	37	34	39	32		

Appendix B
Sample Curriculum Vitae

Jay L. Colbert
Curriculum vitae
October 10, 2018

J. Willard Marriott Library
The University of Utah
295 S 1500 E
2110E
Salt Lake City, UT 84112-0860
Phone: (801) 581-4403
Email: jay.colbert@utah.edu

Education

2017	M.S. Library and Information Science, University of Illinois at Urbana–Champaign
2015	B.A. English, College of William & Mary

Professional Employment

2017	J. Willard Marriott Library, University of Utah, Resident Librarian

Volunteer Experience

2016–2017	University of Illinois LGBT Resource Center, Library Intern
2016	Gerber/Hart Library and Archives, Cataloging Practicum

⊚ Publications

Refereed Journal Articles

2017   Colbert, J. L. (2017). Coming out of the controlled closet: A comparison of patron keywords for queer topics to Library of Congress Subject Headings. *Library Philosophy and Practice.*

2017   Colbert, J. L. (2017). Patron-driven subject access: How librarians can mitigate that "power to name." *In the Library with the Lead Pipe.*

Manuscripts in Preparation

2019   Alston, J., Chiu, A., Colbert, J. L., Rutledge, L. *Developing a residency program: A practical guide for librarians.* Lanham, MD: Rowman & Littlefield.

Other Publications

2017   Colbert, J. L. (2017, April 25). Comparing Library of Congress Subject Headings to keyword searches involving LGBT topics: A pilot study (Thesis). University of Illinois at Urbana-Champaign, Urbana, IL.

⊚ Awards and Honors

2018   Digital Library Federation Forum Students + New Professionals Fellowship
2018   American Library Association 2018 Emerging Leader
2018   EBSCO ALA Annual Conference Sponsorship
2017   Beta Phi Mu
2017   Phi Kappa Phi
2016   Best Poster, BOBCATSSS Conference

⊚ Conference Activity

Presentations

2018   Colbert, J. L. (2018, August 2). *Lost in translation: Information seeking behaviors in first-year students.* Presentation given at the New Librarian Summit. 2018 Conference, San Jose, CA.

Lightning Talks

2017   Colbert, J. L. (2017, October 28). *The limits of subject cataloging media in an LGBTQ collection.* Talk given at the Online Audiovisual Catalogers (OLAC), Inc. 2017 Conference, Richmond, VA.

Posters

2018   Colbert, J. L., Conner-Gaten, A., Ganin, N., Libby, G., & Sorrell, R. (2018, June 22). *Developing a tribal libraries, archives, & museums (TLAMs) directory*. Poster presented at the Annual Library Association (ALA) Annual Conference, New Orleans, LA.

2018   Colbert, J. L., & Sorrell, R. (2018, June 7). *Developing a tribal libraries, archives, & museums (TLAMs) directory*. Poster presented at the Tribal College Librarians Institute (TCLI), Bozeman, MT.

2017   Colbert, J. L. (2017, June 22–27). *Comparing Library of Congress Subject Headings to keyword searches involving LGBT Topics: A pilot study*. Poster presented at the Annual Library Association (ALA) Annual Conference, Chicago, IL.

2016   Colbert, J. L. (2017, January 27–29). *The search that dare not speak its name: LGBT information and catalog records*. Poster presented at the 24th BOB-CATSSS Conference, Lyon, France.

Workshops

2017   Colbert, J. L. (February 17–19). *Finding ourselves in the library: Locating LGBTQ representational materials in libraries*. Workshop presented at the Midwest Bisexual, Lesbian, Gay, Trans, and Ally College Conference (MBLGTACC), Chicago, IL.

2017   Colbert, J. L., & Mills, D. (February 17–19). *Keeping yourself safe online: Privacy basics*. Workshop presented at the Midwest Bisexual, Lesbian, Gay, Trans, and Ally College Conference (MBLGTACC), Chicago, IL.

2016   Colbert, J. L., & Irvine, A. (February 19–21). *Finding ourselves in the library: Finding LGBTQIA representational materials in libraries*. Workshop presented at the Midwest Bisexual, Lesbian, Gay, Trans, and Ally College Conference (MBLGTACC), Lafayette, IN.

⊚ Teaching Experience

LEAP Learning Communities

2018   Engineering LEAP Humanities Seminar: Diversity in American Urban Spaces
 • Library instruction
 • Curriculum development

2017   Engineering LEAP Seminar: Social and Ethical Implications of Engineering
 • Library instruction
 • Curriculum development

⑥ Service to Profession

2018–	Member of the American Library Association's (ALA) Association for Library Collections and Technical Services (ALCTS) Cataloging and Metadata Management Section (CaMMS) Recruitment and Mentoring Committee
2018–	Intern of the Cataloging Policy Committee (CAPC) of the Online Audiovisual Catalogers, Inc. (OLAC)
2018–	Member of the Subject Authority Cooperative Program (SACO) Latin America and Indigenous Peoples of the Americas Funnel
2017–	Member of the Video Game Genre Headings Working Group of the American Library Association's (ALA) Association for Library Collections and Technical Services (ALCTS) Subject Analysis (SAC) Subcommittee for Genre/Form Implementation (GFIS)
2016–2018	Member of the Resources Committee of the Gay, Lesbian, Bisexual, and Transgender (GLBT) Round Table of the American Library Association (ALA)

⑥ Departmental/University Service

2017–	Graduate Student Services Committee
2017–2018	Digital Curation Librarian Search Committee

⑥ Media Coverage

2018	Malden, C. (2018, May 7). EBSCO and ALA award seven scholarships enabling librarians to attend 2018 Annual Conference [Text]. Retrieved July 5, 2018, from http://www.ala.org/news/press-releases/2018/05/ebsco-and-ala-award-seven-scholarships-enabling-librarians-attend-2018-annual.
2018	Morehart, P. (2018, May 1). Emerging Leaders 2018. *American Libraries Magazine, 49*(5). Retrieved from https://americanlibrariesmagazine.org/2018/05/01/emerging- leaders-2018/.
2018	Anderson, E. (2018, March 29). Wikipedia edit-a-thon at Marriott Library increases woman representation on the site. Retrieved October 2, 2018, from http://dailyutahchronicle.com/2018/03/29/wikipedia-edit-a-thon-at-marriott-library-increases-woman-representation-on-the-site/.
2018	Calvin, B. (2017, December 1). New class of 2018 Emerging Leaders announced [Text]. Retrieved March 1, 2018, from http://www.ala.org/news/member-news/2017/12/new- class-2018-emerging-leaders-announced.

⑥ Related Professional Skills

Controlled Vocabulary and Classification Schemes

Art & Architecture Thesaurus
Dewey Decimal Classification

Library of Congress Classification
Library of Congress Subject Headings
NACO trained

Library Software

Alma
EndNote
MARCEdit
Mendeley
OASIS
OCLC Connexion
OpenRefine
Voyager
Zotero

Metadata Schema and Encoding Standards

Categories for the Description of Works of Art (CDWA) Lite
Encoded Archival Description (EAD)
Data Documentation Initiative (DDI)
Dublin Core
MAchine Readable Cataloging (MARC)
Metadata Encoding and Transmission Standard (METS)
Metadata Object Description Schema (MODS)
Public Broadcasting Metadata Dictionary (PBCore)
Preservation Metadata: Implementation Strategies (PREMIS)
Resource Description and Access (RDA)
eXtensible Markup Language (XML)
eXtensible Stylesheet Language (XSL)

Research

ATLAS.ti
Qualitative research methods

Semantic Web

BIBFRAME
Friend of a Friend (FOAF)
Resource Description Framework (RDF) and RDF Schema (RDFS)
Simple Knowledge Organization System (SKOS)
Turtle
Web Ontology Language (OWL)

Languages

Arabic   beginner, can transliterate with dictionary
English   native

French	can read with dictionary
German	good
Japanese	Hiragana and Katakana pronunciation and transliteration with dictionary only
Māori	pronunciation only

⊚ Professional Memberships

American Indian Library Association(AILA)
American Library Association (ALA)

- Association for Library Collections and Technical Services (ALCTS)
  - Cataloging and Metadata Management Section
- Association of College and Research Libraries (ACRL)
  - Residency Interest Group
  - Technical Services Interest Group
  - University Libraries Section
- Gay, Lesbian, Bisexual, and Transgender (GLBT) Round Table

Online Audiovisual Catalogers (OLAC), Inc.

Appendix C

Sample Residency Job Advertisement from GVSU

GRAND VALLEY STATE UNIVERSITY LIBRARIES are hiring for a three-year Library Faculty Fellow as part of the ACRL Diversity Alliance. Please share widely!

Annie Bélanger
March 2018
Job Title: Library Faculty Diversity Fellow
Location: Allendale Campus

Grand Valley State University Libraries seeks applications for a 2018–2020 Library Faculty Diversity Fellow. This three-year faculty position provides an opportunity for a newly graduated librarian, with a demonstrated commitment to diversity, equity, and inclusion, to gain professional experience as an academic librarian and faculty member. The Libraries seek to hire for growth with a focus on being a self-starter with confident humility and curiosity as well as strong time management skills, while we commit to growing digital and research skills.

The fellow will gain meaningful work experience in GVSU Libraries with a focus on digital projects and services, including open data, open scholarship, scholarly communications and publishing, data visualization, and related initiatives. Serving as the experimental lead for digital scholarship service exploration with mentoring and support from other librarians, the fellow will gain project management and service assessment experience. The fellow will have the opportunity to work with librarians in the other departments and participate in projects to gain experience in the areas that pique their interests through a rotation program. Close collaboration with faculty in the libraries and the university will be emphasized.

The fellowship will offer many opportunities for professional development: The fellow will be encouraged to deliver presentations, attend national and regional conferences, and write for professional publications. Financial support for professional development opportunities will be provided. The fellow will serve on library committees as appropriate and participate in the Libraries' mentoring program.

GVSU Libraries are committed to building a culturally diverse workplace and strongly encourage applications from minority candidates, candidates with disabilities, and those with experience working on accessibility or inclusion initiatives. Information about salaries, professional development, and more can be found at https://www.gvsu.edu/library/job-opportunities-at-gvsu-libraries-faq-51.htm. For more information on GVSU Libraries, please visit http://gvsu.edu/libraries.

Minimum Qualifications

- (Expected or earned in the past year) Master's degree from a program accredited by the American Library Association (ALA) or from a program in a country with a formal accreditation process as identified by ALA
- Excellent interpersonal and communication skills
- Demonstrated ability to work independently and collaboratively in a team environment
- Strong collaboration skills
- Commitment to equity, diversity, and inclusion as well as a focus on user needs and experience
- Strong interpersonal skills, such as confident humility and the ability to interact with others with respect and empathy
- Confident humility—able to balance the need for confidence in order to successfully advocate with others' expertise and values
- Self-starter—ability to identify needed work and pursue it in line with strategic directions
- Curiosity—ability to self-identify the need for new skills/knowledge and pursue acquiring them

Desired Qualifications

- Understanding of project leadership and/or management
- Ability to design and deliver training
- Completed coursework and/or experience in one of the following: text-mining, digital humanities, digital scholarship, computer sciences, web coding, GIS or related initiatives

Department/Division: University Libraries
Campus: Allendale
Salary: Commensurate with experience and qualifications
Application Deadline Date: TDB
How to Apply: Applications accepted online only at jobs.gvsu.edu. Please include a cover letter, resume, statement of impact or commitment to inclusion, and at least two references with name, address, telephone, and e-mail address. The online application will allow you to attach these and other relevant supporting documents electronically. If you have questions or need assistance, call Human Resources at 616-331-2215.
Questions? Feel free to contact Annie Bélanger, search committee chair via e-mail [redacted].

Grand Valley State University is guided by values for inclusiveness and community which are integral to our mission to educate students to shape their lives, their professions, and their societies, and to enrich the community through excellent teaching, active scholarship, and public service. The University is an affirmative action, equal opportunity institution. It encourages diversity and provides equal opportunity in education, employment, all of its programs, and the use of its facilities. Members of the University community, including candidates for employment or admissions, and visitors or guests have the right to be free from acts of harassment and discrimination, including sexual misconduct, which are prohibited if they discriminate or harass on the basis of age, color, disability, familial status, height, marital status, national origin, political affiliation, race, religion, sex/gender (including gender identity and expression), sexual orientation, veteran or active duty military status, or weight. The University will provide reasonable accommodations to qualified individuals with disabilities. See www.gvsu.edu/affirmative/. [Include the following for job advertisements:] TDD Callers: Call Michigan Relay Center 1-800-649-3777.

Appendix D

Sample Proposals for Residency Rotations from GVSU

GRAND VALLEY
STATE UNIVERSITY
UNIVERSITY LIBRARIES

⊚ ACRL Diversity Alliance—Preparing New Library Faculty—Proposals for Rotations

Annie Bélanger for Library Council
March 2018
Diversity Alliance Residency Program
   The ACRL Diversity Alliance residency program creates positions that will increase the numbers of opportunities for professionally underrepresented groups. The positions will be three years in lengths as visiting faculty librarians at GVSU libraries.

Background/Context

"The ACRL Diversity Alliance program unites academic libraries who share a commitment to increase the hiring pipeline of qualified, talented individuals from underrepresented racial and ethnic groups. By thinking bigger and broader, across all academic libraries, we will introduce and welcome to the job market underrepresented racial and ethnic groups with work experiences that advance academic/research libraries.

   The commitment of each library leader to create one or more residency positions will increase the numbers of opportunities for professionally underrepresented racial and ethnic groups to gain the knowledge, skills and competencies to thrive in an academic context. Participation in the ACRL Diversity Alliance requires a deep commitment on the part of library leaders to open doors, share their networks, connect people at conferences, etc., to facilitate deeper understanding of the profession and prepare them to participate in the wider higher education community and for success in scholarship, professional service, and leadership. In addition to the network of library leaders, residents will have access to a cohort and/or network that allows for sharing of ideas, resources, best practices, etc."[1]

GVSU Libraries participation in the ACRL Diversity Alliance furthers the inclusive values outlined in our 2016–2021 strategic plan. This pilot program at GVSU would allow us to explore this project long term while allowing us to experiment with emerging needs and trends in our field.

Timeline

We would like to start the first two residents in Spring/Summer 2018 to align with new library science graduates as they begin to look for work experience. The second resident will begin either in December 2018 or Spring/Summer 2019, depending on funding. Residents would have a three-year appointment.

Scope and Deliverables

Each resident would have his or her work load split in the following way:

- A rotation through areas and departments at GVSU libraries, exposing residents to multiple areas throughout the profession: 40%
- A focus project/responsibility providing exposure to a specific area of library science that is also a current need at GVSU libraries: 40%
- Scholarly/creative activity: 10%
- Service: 5%
- Professional development through collaboration with other regional ACRL Diversity Alliance participants for strategic topic daylong institutes (examples could include: project management, user experience, vendor negotiations, etc.): 5%

Rotation/Project Proposal Criteria

A significant importance of the residency program is to expose the resident(s) to the richness of the field of librarianship and the opportunities to gain knowledge offered in the different areas. The creation of variety and deep skill building in the program is important to ensure that the resident will be competitive in searches by the end of the second year of the residency program and to increase the likelihood of persistence in the field.

To identify a rotation possibility, articulate:

- Knowledge/skills area development
- Timeline for learning
- Time commitment required on a weekly basis
- Focus statement (1–2 paragraphs) indicating what the resident can expect to do
- Mentor(s)
- Training needed/availability

This will be used to develop the portfolios available for rotations and prioritize them based on institutional need as well.

ⓖ Samples from the University of Virginia Library[2] of a Public-Facing Output

Residency in Scholarly Communication

A solid example that articulates what he/she will do and what he/she will learn.

The resident in Scholarly Communication will work in open publishing, open access, changes in subscription models, author rights, and preservation of the scholarly record. By open access, we mean "literature that is digital, online, free of charge, and free of most copyright and licensing restrictions." The Resident will closely work with faculty-authors, liaison (subject) librarians, and others active in this sphere. The resident will create and disseminate open access talking points that resonate with faculty and staff, draft recommendations on how the library can more effectively communicate its Scholarly Communications services and policies, and identify the necessary resources to better support and advocate for new models of open scholarship. The resident will have deep knowledge of issues and approaches necessary to lead library scholarly communication efforts.

UX (User Experience)

This team leverages methods (focus groups, usability studies, feedback mechanisms) and assessments to define, shape, and prioritize Library physical and online services. It offers methods to support library projects, manages the public and staff content management systems and websites incorporating the University brand elements, website information architecture, designs, and develops accessible/inclusive user interaction (UI) for all online services and works closely with communication to offer internal staff newsletter, emergency messaging, library service information, and digital and physical signage.

Resident Librarian for Library Information Technology (LIT)

This example would require significant development to be considered.

LIT works collaboratively with the Library, the University, and the higher education community to provide cost-effective and accessible solutions for hardware, software (licensed and open source), and user experience. The resident librarian would join thirty-six engineers, librarians, and students organized into four teams: User Experience (UX), Scholarly Access Technologies (SAT), Space and Infrastructure Technologies (SIT), and Digital Content Management & Dissemination (DCMD).

ⓖ Notes

1. Information pulled from www.ala.org/acrl/issues/diversityalliance.
2. Access online at www.library.virginia.edu/resident-librarian/.

Appendix E

Sample Rotations for a Resident Librarian from GVSU

ACRL Rotation 2018/2019
Updated July 2018

Operation and User Services Department

During the User Experience (UX) rotation, the resident will gain an understanding of library user experience from a theoretical perspective as well as practical, hands-on experience developing and implementing UX techniques focused on improving UX within physical spaces and services. This may include learning about design thinking, appreciative inquiry, journey mapping, ethnographic user research, and feedback channel analysis. The resident will first become familiar with service desk environments and participate in UX team initiatives across locations. Building upon knowledge gained in this initial exposure to UX work, the resident will have an opportunity to lead a UX project from discovery to implementation, supported by the UX Librarian.

Note: For the most meaningful experience, this rotation should be completed in Fall and Winter semesters and not during Spring/Summer.

Systems and Technology

The resident in Systems and Technology will develop and run usability tests, conduct user research, and review usage analytics of library websites. The resident will closely work with the User Experience Librarian, the Library Applications Developer, the Instructional Design Librarian, and others. The resident will recommend design and content changes to improve the user experience based on user research and tests but will not be responsible for implementing changes. The resident will have deep knowledge of the issues and approaches necessary to lead library user experience initiatives.

Research in Professional Programs—Ithaka S+R Research Project

The resident in Professional Programs will work with a liaison librarian on a qualitative research project with the business college and sponsored by Ithaka S+R. The resident will conduct local research with faculty and instructors who teach courses in business. Approximately fifteen interviews will take place in Fall 2018. The resident, along with the research team, will transcribe and code the interviews and prepare a local report for Ithaka S+R. Ithaka will review the findings of all participating institutions and prepare a public capstone report. The resident will have deep knowledge of qualitative research methods and the experience of authoring a local report.

Instruction Rotation

This three-month rotation will give the fellow an introduction to instructional best practices in both online and in-person teaching environments. The resident will be introduced to some introductory readings (depending on previous experience) and will observe different library instructors teach followed by guided debriefing meetings to build knowledge and skills in this area during the first few weeks of the rotation. The fellow will also meet with the WRT 150 coordinator to learn the background and context for the Libraries' support of WRT 150.

The ultimate goal for the in-person portion of the rotation will be to partner with a classroom instructor on integrating a library session (or sessions) into a WRT 150 section. The resident will be paired with an instruction mentor to form the session(s).

For the online component, the resident would be paired with our Instructional Design Librarian to develop an online learning object to support one of the standardized learning outcomes for WRT 150. The training for this would be a deep partnership with the Instructional Design Librarian to go over the Instructional Design Model, learning a creation software, accessibility best practices, and prototyping a learning object.

The resident would be encouraged to attend WRT 150 instructor meetings and any relevant FTLC trainings they thought might further develop this skill area.

(January or August: intro to teaching and WRT 150, February or September: collaborate with in-person instruction, March/November: collaborate on an online learning object)

Liaison Rotation

This semester rotation would start with a series of one-on-one meetings with the current liaisons with a standard set of questions to learn different approaches to the position and the disciplinary idiosyncrasies that occur in the work.

Upon completion of the introductory meetings with liaisons, the resident will partner with a specific liaison librarian. They will review and revise an instructional plan, they will work with a liaison on a collection management project (database renewal, database overlap analysis, explore trends in purchasing behavior for approval plan parameters, etc.), and the resident will take the lead on the development of an outreach campaign to promote a library service, in collaboration with others in the Libraries (OER adoption, data management, etc.). The resident will partner with liaison department heads to develop an assessment of the outreach approach for future iterations.

This rotation could run the course of a semester, starting with meetings with the liaisons in the first month and diving into the other projects, with some time for individual skill building of one per month. (September/January: env. scan, October/February: outreach, November/March: instruction plan, December/April: collections)

Appendix F
Authors' Research Results

WE DESIGNED AND DISTRIBUTED a Qualtrics survey in the spring of 2018 with the goal of collecting data from persons belonging to any of four specific demographics: former resident librarians, current resident librarians, former residency coordinators, and current residency coordinators. The questions were designed so that the same concepts were being investigated from the perspective of residents and coordinators. Ultimately, a primary objective was to determine if there were significant differences in how well-executed residents thought certain components of the residency were compared to how well-executed coordinators thought those components of the residency were. There was not enough survey data to make generalizable conclusions, so only the descriptive statistical results are found here. Only two individuals proceeded with the survey while identifying themselves as former residency coordinators, so tables are not included for former residency coordinators.

Table F.1. Current Residency Coordinator Survey Responses to Questions on Resident Projects and Skills

	I CONSULT WITH THE RESIDENT(S) ABOUT THEIR PROJECTS	I CONSULT WITH THE RESIDENT(S) ABOUT SKILLS THEY NEED TO LEARN OR IMPROVE ON	THE RESIDENT CHOOSES PROJECTS ACCORDING TO THEIR INTERESTS
Strongly Agree	6 (67%)	6 (67%)	4 (44%)
Agree	1 (11%)	2 (22%)	3 (34%)
Somewhat Agree	2 (22%)	1 (11%)	2 (22%)
Neither Agree nor Disagree	0 (0%)	0 (0%)	0 (0%)
Somewhat Disagree	0 (0%)	0 (0%)	0 (0%)
Disagree	0 (0%)	0 (0%)	0 (0%)
Strongly Disagree	0 (0%)	0 (0%)	0 (0%)

Table F.2. Current Residency Coordinator Survey Responses to Questions Regarding Library Employee Support of the Residency Program (n=9)

	LIBRARY ADMINISTRATORS DEMONSTRATE SUPPORT FOR THE RESIDENCY PROGRAM	LIBRARIANS DEMONSTRATE SUPPORT FOR THE RESIDENCY PROGRAM	OTHER LIBRARY STAFF DEMONSTRATE SUPPORT FOR THE RESIDENCY PROGRAM
Strongly Agree	6 (67%)	3 (33%)	3 (33%)
Agree	2 (22%)	5 (56%)	4 (45%)
Somewhat Agree	1 (11%)	1 (11%)	2 (22%)
Neither Agree nor Disagree	0 (0%)	0 (0%)	0 (0%)
Somewhat Disagree	0 (0%)	0 (0%)	0 (0%)
Disagree	0 (0%)	0 (0%)	0 (0%)
Strongly Disagree	0 (0%)	0 (0%)	0 (0%)

Table F.3. Current Residency Coordinator Survey Responses to Questions Regarding Library Employee Support of the Residents (n=9)

	LIBRARY ADMINISTRATORS SUPPORT THE RESIDENT(S)	LIBRARIANS SUPPORT THE RESIDENT(S)	OTHER LIBRARY STAFF SUPPORT THE RESIDENT(S)
Strongly Agree	3 (67%)	3 (33%)	3 (33%)
Agree	5 (22%)	5 (56%)	5 (45%)
Somewhat Agree	1 (11%)	1 (11%)	1 (22%)
Neither Agree nor Disagree	0 (0%)	0 (0%)	0 (0%)
Somewhat Disagree	0 (0%)	0 (0%)	0 (0%)
Disagree	0 (0%)	0 (0%)	0 (0%)
Strongly Disagree	0 (0%)	0 (0%)	0 (0%)

Table F.4. Current Residency Coordinator Survey Responses to Questions Regarding Residency Assessment

	DO YOU HAVE A FORMAL ASSESSMENT PLAN IN PLACE FOR THE RESIDENCY? (N=9)	DO YOU DO ANY FORM OF AD HOC ASSESSMENT? (N=5)
Yes	5 (55%)	5 (100%)
No	4 (45%)	0 (0%)

Table F.5. Current Residency Coordinator Survey Responses Indicating Level of Agreement with Statements About Assessment (n=4)

	I USE THE FORMAL ASSESSMENT PLAN THAT WAS DEVELOPED AND IN PLACE	I CONSULTED WITH THE RESIDENT(S) IN FINALIZING THE ASSESSMENT PLAN	I MAKE CHANGES TO THE PROGRAM BASED ON ASSESSMENT RESULTS	THE ASSESSMENT PLAN IS USEFUL	I MODIFY THE ASSESSMENT PLAN AS NEEDED
A Great Deal	3 (75%)	1 (25%)	2 (50%)	2 (50%)	1 (25%)
A Lot	0 (0%)	1 (25%)	1 (25%)	2 (50%)	1 (25%)
A Moderate Amount	1 (25%)	1 (25%)	1 (25%)	0 (0%)	1 (25%)
A Little	0 (0%)	0 (0%)	0 (0%)	0 (0%)	1 (25%)
Not At All	0 (0%)	1 (25%)	0 (0%)	0 (0%)	0 (0%)

Table F.6. Current Residency Coordinator Responses to Whether or Not Resident Salary and Related Expenses Are Written into the Institutional Budget (n=9)

	IS THE RESIDENT(S)'S SALARY AND ANY OTHER RELATED EXPENSES WRITTEN INTO THE INSTITUTION'S BUDGET?
Yes	7 (78%)
No	2 (22%)

Table F.7. Current Coordinator Responses When Asked if They Are Currently Coordinating Their Institution's First Residency Program

	ARE YOU CURRENTLY COORDINATING YOUR INSTITUTION'S FIRST RESIDENCY PROGRAM?
Yes	4 (45%)
No	5 (55%)
Other	0

Table F.8. Current Coordinator Identification of What Type of Residency They Coordinate (respondents could select multiple answers)

WHAT TYPE OF RESIDENCY ARE YOU COORDINATING? SELECT ALL THAT APPLY.	
Single resident	5
Cohort residency (more than one concurrent resident)	2
Diversity residency	3
Function-specific residency (focus on one functional area, duty, or subject within the library)	1
Holistic/rotation residency (the resident(s) "rotate" in multiple departments of the library or have multiple duties designed to give a holistic overview of librarianship)	5
Academic library residency	6
Public library residency	1
Other (please specify)	2

Table F.9. Term Length of Residency as Indicated by Current Residency Coordinators (n=9)

WHAT IS THE TERM DURATION OF THE RESIDENCY PROGRAM?	
Less than 1 year	1 (11%)
1 year	0
1–2 years	3 (33%)
2 years	3 (33%)
Greater than 2 years	2 (23%)

Table F.10. Current Resident Survey Responses to Questions on Resident Projects and Skills (n=17)

	I AM CONSULTED WITH ABOUT PROJECTS.	I RECEIVE ADVICE ABOUT SKILLS I SHOULD LEARN OR IMPROVE UPON.	I CHOOSE PROJECTS ACCORDING TO MY INTERESTS.
Strongly Agree	4 (24%)	3 (18%)	3 (18%)
Agree	7 (40%)	6 (34%)	6 (34%)
Somewhat Agree	4 (24%)	3 (18%)	4 (24%)
Neither Agree nor Disagree	2 (12%)	1 (6%)	2 (12%)
Somewhat Disagree	0 (0%)	1 (6%)	0 (0%)
Disagree	0 (0%)	0 (0%)	1 (6%)
Strongly Disagree	0 (0%)	3 (18%)	1 (6%)

Table F.11. Current Resident Survey Responses to Questions Regarding Library Employee Support of the Residency Program

	LIBRARY ADMINISTRATORS DEMONSTRATE SUPPORT FOR THE RESIDENCY PROGRAM (N=17)	LIBRARIANS DEMONSTRATE SUPPORT FOR THE RESIDENCY PROGRAM (N=16)	OTHER LIBRARY STAFF DEMONSTRATE SUPPORT FOR THE RESIDENCY PROGRAM (N=16)
Strongly Agree	10 (59%)	7 (44%)	5 (31%)
Agree	3 (17%)	5 (31%)	4 (25%)
Somewhat Agree	0 (0%)	2 (13%)	0 (0%)
Neither Agree nor Disagree	2 (12%)	1 (6%)	5 (31%)
Somewhat Disagree	2 (12%)	1 (6%)	2 (13%)
Disagree	0 (0%)	0 (0%)	0 (0%)
Strongly Disagree	0 (0%)	0 (0%)	0 (0%)

Table F.12. Current Resident Survey Responses to Questions Regarding Library Employee Support of the Residents (n=17)

	LIBRARY ADMINISTRATORS SUPPORT ME	LIBRARIANS SUPPORT ME	OTHER LIBRARY STAFF SUPPORT ME
Strongly Agree	6 (35%)	7 (41%)	4 (23%)
Agree	6 (35%)	7 (41%)	6 (35%)
Somewhat Agree	3 (18%)	2 (12%)	3 (18%)
Neither Agree nor Disagree	0 (0%)	0 (0%)	3 (18%)
Somewhat Disagree	2 (12%)	1 (6%)	1 (6%)
Disagree	0 (0%)	0 (0%)	0 (0%)
Strongly Disagree	0 (0%)	0 (0%)	0 (0%)

Table F.13. Current Resident Survey Responses to Questions Regarding Residency Assessment

	DOES YOU INSTITUTION HAVE A FORMAL ASSESSMENT PLAN IN PLACE FOR THE RESIDENCY? (N=16)	DOES YOUR INSTITUTION DO ANY FORM OF AD HOC ASSESSMENT? (N=5)
Yes	7 (44%)	2 (40%)
No	9 (56%)	3 (60%)

Table F.14. Current Resident Survey Responses Indicating Level of Agreement with Statements About Assessment (n=7)

	THE FORMAL ASSESSMENT PLAN THAT WAS DEVELOPED AND IN PLACE IS BEING USED.	I AM CONSULTED WITH IN FINALIZING THE ASSESSMENT PLAN.	CHANGES ARE MADE TO THE RESIDENCY PROGRAM BASED ON ASSESSMENT RESULTS.	THE ASSESSMENT PLAN IS USEFUL.	THE ASSESSMENT PLAN IS MODIFIED AS NEEDED.
Strongly Agree	2 (29%)	4 (58%)	1 (13%)	3 (42%)	3 (43%)
Agree	2 (29%)	2 (29%)	3 (43%)	2 (29%)	4 (57%)
Somewhat Agree	3 (42%)	1 (13%)	1 (13%)	2 (29%)	0 (0%)
Neither Agree nor Disagree	0 (0%)	0 (0%)	2 (29%)	0 (0%)	0 (0%)
Somewhat Disagree	0 (0%)	0 (0%)	0 (0%)	0 (0%)	0 (0%)
Disagree	0 (0%)	0 (0%)	0 (0%)	0 (0%)	0 (0%)
Strongly Disagree	0 (0%)	0 (0%)	0 (0%)	0 (0%)	0 (0%)

Table F.15. Current Residency Coordinator Responses to Whether or Not Resident Salary and Related Expenses Are Written into the Institutional Budget (n=17)

	IS YOUR SALARY AND ANY OTHER RELATED EXPENSES WRITTEN INTO THE INSTITUTION'S BUDGET?
Yes	9 (53%)
No	1 (5%)
I Don't Know	7 (42%)

Table F.16. Current Resident Responses When Asked if They Are Their Institution's First Resident (n=17)

	ARE YOU YOUR INSTITUTION'S FIRST RESIDENT?
Yes	4 (23%)
No	12 (71%)
Other	1 (6%)

Table F.17. Current Resident Identification of What Type of Residency They Are In (respondents could select multiple answers)

WHAT TYPE OF RESIDENCY ARE YOU A RESIDENT OF? SELECT ALL THAT APPLY.	
Single resident	5
Cohort residency (more than one concurrent resident)	11
Diversity residency	9
Function-specific residency (focus on one functional area, duty, or subject within the library)	6
Holistic/rotation residency (the resident(s) "rotate" in multiple departments of the library or have multiple duties designed to give a holistic overview of librarianship)	6
Academic library residency	13
Public library residency	0
Other (please specify)	0

Table F.18. Term Length of Residency as Indicated by Former Residents (n=22)

WHAT IS THE TERM DURATION OF THE RESIDENCY PROGRAM?	
Less than 1 year	1 (6%)
1 year	3 (18%)
1–2 years	3 (18%)
2 years	4 (24%)
Greater than 2 years	6 (34%)

Table F.19. Current Resident Survey Responses to Questions Regarding Library Employee Support of the Residency Program (n=17)

	LIBRARY ADMINISTRATORS UNDERSTAND THE PURPOSE OF THE RESIDENCY.	LIBRARIANS UNDERSTAND THE PURPOSE OF THE RESIDENCY.	OTHER LIBRARY STAFF UNDERSTAND THE PURPOSE OF THE RESIDENCY.
Strongly Agree	7 (41%)	6 (34%)	3 (17%)
Agree	5 (29%)	4 (24%)	2 (12%)
Somewhat Agree	3 (18%)	4 (24%)	4 (24%)
Neither Agree nor Disagree	1 (6%)	0 (0%)	1 (6%)
Somewhat Disagree	1 (6%)	2 (12%)	3 (17%)
Disagree	0 (0%)	1 (6%)	2 (12%)
Strongly Disagree	0 (0%)	0 (0%)	2 (12%)

Table F.20. Former Resident Survey Responses to Questions on Resident Projects and Skills (n=22)

	I WAS CONSULTED WITH ABOUT PROJECTS.	I RECEIVED ADVICE ABOUT SKILLS I SHOULD LEARN OR IMPROVE UPON.	I CHOSE PROJECTS ACCORDING TO MY INTERESTS.
Strongly Agree	7 (31%)	9 (41%)	11 (50%)
Agree	9 (40%)	2 (9%)	6 (27%)
Somewhat Agree	5 (23%)	7 (31%)	2 (9%)
Neither Agree nor Disagree	0 (0%)	1 (5%)	2 (9%)
Somewhat Disagree	0 (0%)	1 (5%)	0 (0%)
Disagree	0 (0%)	1 (5%)	0 (0%)
Strongly Disagree	1 (5%)	1 (5%)	1 (5%)

Table F.21. Former Resident Survey Responses to Questions Regarding Library Employee Support of the Residency Program (n=21)

	LIBRARY ADMINISTRATORS DEMONSTRATED SUPPORT FOR THE RESIDENCY PROGRAM.	LIBRARIANS DEMONSTRATED SUPPORT FOR THE RESIDENCY PROGRAM.	OTHER LIBRARY STAFF DEMONSTRATED SUPPORT FOR THE RESIDENCY PROGRAM.
Strongly Agree	12 (57%)	9 (43%)	6 (29%)
Agree	2 (9%)	5 (24%)	4 (19%)
Somewhat Agree	4 (19%)	4 (19%)	3 (14%)
Neither Agree nor Disagree	1 (5%)	0 (0%)	3 (14%)
Somewhat Disagree	2 (9%)	1 (5%)	3 (14%)
Disagree	0 (0%)	2 (9%)	2 (9%)
Strongly Disagree	0 (0%)	0 (0%)	0 (0%)

Table F.22. Former Resident Survey Responses to Questions Regarding Library Employee Support of the Residents (n=21)

	LIBRARY ADMINISTRATORS SUPPORTED ME.	LIBRARIANS SUPPORTED ME.	OTHER LIBRARY STAFF SUPPORTED ME.
Strongly Agree	11 (52%)	11 (52%)	8 (38%)
Agree	4 (19%)	6 (29%)	4 (19%)
Somewhat Agree	3 (14%)	0 (0%)	3 (14%)
Neither Agree nor Disagree	1 (5%)	1 (5%)	2 (9%)
Somewhat Disagree	0 (0%)	0 (0%)	1 (6%)
Disagree	1 (5%)	3 (14%)	3 (14%)
Strongly Disagree	1 (5%)	0 (0%)	0 (0%)

Table F.23. Former Resident Survey Responses to Questions Regarding Residency Assessment

	DID YOUR INSTITUTION HAVE A FORMAL ASSESSMENT PLAN IN PLACE FOR THE RESIDENCY? (N=16)	DID YOUR INSTITUTION DO ANY FORM OF AD HOC ASSESSMENT? (N=6)
Yes	5 (31%)	3 (50%)
No	11 (69%)	3 (50%)

Table F.24. Former Resident Survey Responses Indicating Level of Agreement with Statements About Assessment (n=5)

	THE FORMAL ASSESSMENT PLAN THAT WAS DEVELOPED AND IN PLACE WAS BEING USED.	I AM CONSULTED WITH IN FINALIZING THE ASSESSMENT PLAN	CHANGES WERE MADE TO THE RESIDENCY PROGRAM BASED ON ASSESSMENT RESULTS.	THE ASSESSMENT PLAN WAS USEFUL.	THE ASSESSMENT PLAN WAS MODIFIED AS NEEDED.
Strongly Agree	0 (0%)	0 (0%)	0 (0%)	0 (0%)	0 (0%)
Agree	2 (40%)	1 (20%)	0 (0%)	0 (0%)	0 (0%)
Somewhat Agree	2 (40%)	0 (0%)	1 (20%)	4 (80%)	2 (40%)
Neither Agree nor Disagree	0 (0%)	0 (0%)	2 (40%)	0 (0%)	1 (20%)
Somewhat Disagree	0 (0%)	1 (20%)	1 (20%)	0 (0%)	0 (0%)
Disagree	1 (20%)	1 (20%)	0 (0%)	1 (20%)	2 (40%)
Strongly Disagree	0 (0%)	2 (40%)	1 (20%)	0 (0%)	0 (0%)

Table F.25. Current Residency Coordinator Responses to Whether or Not Resident Salary and Related Expenses Are Written into the Institutional Budget (n=22)

	WAS YOUR SALARY AND ANY OTHER RELATED EXPENSES WRITTEN INTO THE INSTITUTION'S BUDGET?
Yes	11 (50%)
No	3 (14%)
I Don't Know	8 (36%)

Table F.26. Former Resident Responses When Asked if They Are Their Institution's First Resident (n=23)

	WERE YOU YOUR INSTITUTION'S FIRST RESIDENT?
Yes	5 (22%)
No	18 (78%)
Other	0 (0%)

Table F.27. Current Resident Identification of What Type of Residency They Are In (respondents could select multiple answers)

WHAT TYPE OF RESIDENCY WERE YOU A RESIDENT OF? SELECT ALL THAT APPLY.	
Single resident	9
Cohort residency (more than one concurrent resident)	10
Diversity residency	12
Function-specific residency (focus on one functional area, duty, or subject within the library)	5
Holistic/rotation residency (the resident(s) "rotate" in multiple departments of the library or have multiple duties designed to give a holistic overview of librarianship)	10
Academic library residency	19
Public library residency	1
Other (please specify)	1

Table F.28. Term Length of Residency as Indicated by Former Residents (n=22)

WHAT IS THE TERM DURATION OF THE RESIDENCY PROGRAM?	
Less than 1 year	1 (5%)
1 year	4 (18%)
1–2 years	1 (5%)
2 years	11 (50%)
Greater than 2 years	5 (22%)

Table F.29. Former Resident Survey Responses to Questions Regarding Library Employee Support of the Residency Program (n=22)

	LIBRARY ADMINISTRATORS UNDERSTOOD THE PURPOSE OF THE RESIDENCY.	LIBRARIANS UNDERSTOOD THE PURPOSE OF THE RESIDENCY.	OTHER LIBRARY STAFF UNDERSTOOD THE PURPOSE OF THE RESIDENCY.
Strongly Agree	8 (36%)	6 (28%)	2 (9%)
Agree	8 (36%)	8 (36%)	6 (28%)
Somewhat Agree	2 (9%)	3 (13%)	6 (28%)
Neither Agree nor Disagree	1 (5%)	0 (0%)	1 (5%)
Somewhat Disagree	2 (9%)	2 (9%)	4 (18%)
Disagree	1 (5%)	1 (5%)	2 (9%)
Strongly Disagree	0 (0%)	2 (9%)	1 (5%)

Index

Malacca Straits, 4, 112
Mao, 103, 105, 106, 107
Marshall Plan, 75
Massachusetts Institute of Technology, 19, 147, 155, 189
Middle East, 3, 4, 56, 70, 71, 73, 77, 168, 177

national oil companies (NOCs), 4, 7, 55, 109, 123, 124, 131, 132, 164
National Security Strategy, 79
North Atlantic Treaty Organization (NATO), 73, 107
NSC-68, 31
nuclear power, 6

Opium War, 104
Organization for Petroleum Exporting Countries (OPEC), 55, 74
Organization for Economic Cooperation and Development (OECD), 12, 53, 59, 74, 131

People's Liberation Army Navy (PLAN), 133, 134, 171, 172, 178
Persian Gulf, 65, 80, 97, 177
Politburo Standing Committee (PSC), 4
Posen, Barry, 27, 33, 41
price reporting agencies (PRAs), 64, 87
principal components analysis (PCA), 15, 145, 146, 186

Qatar, 50

Realism, 28, 76
renewables, 43

return on average capital employed (ROACE), 86, 87, 162, 163
Royal Dutch Shell, 105
Russia, 10, 56, 62, 125, 172

Saudi Arabia, 73, 83, 94
Sea Lines of Communication (SLOCs), 3, 13, 77, 134, 170, 171, 172, 175, 180, 181, 191
shale, 122, 164
SINOPEC, 4
South China Sea, 4, 112, 191
Soviet Union, 28, 30, 38, 78, 105–106, 109, 170
Standard Oil, 70, 84
state-owned enterprises (SOEs), 4
Stockholm International Peace Research Institute, 19
Strait of Hormuz, 61
strategic petroleum reserve (SPR), 74, 131

total primary energy consumption (TPEC), 10, 16, 153
total primary energy supply (TPES), 13
Trans-Pacific Partnership (TPP), 34

United Nations, 16, 17; Comtrade, 17

Very Large Crude Carrier (VLCC), 97, 176

West Texas Intermediate (WTI), 17, 88–91, 127, 164
World War One, 70, 174
World War Two, 5, 7, 69, 71, 77, 80, 105, 174

Yergin, Daniel, 49–50, 53–54, 168, 187